Saltwater, Sweetwater

*Women Write from
California's North Coast*

Collected by *Barbara L. Baer* & *Maureen Anne Jennings*

Floreant Press
Forestville, California

Floreant Press

6195 Anderson Road

Forestville, California 95436

Copyright © 1998 by Floreant Press

Printed in the USA by Floreant Press

10 9 8 7 6 5 4 3 2 1

First Printing

Saltwater, Sweetwater: Women Write from California's North Coast:
  edited by Barbara L. Baer and Maureen Anne Jennings—1st ed.
    p. cm.
    Preassigned LCCN: 97-61562
    ISBN 0-9649497-1-7

        1. American literature—California—Sonoma County.
    2. American literature—California—Mendocino County.
    3. American literature—Women authors. 4. Women—Sonoma
    County (Calif.)—Literary collections. 5. Women—Mendocino
    County (Calif.)—Literary collections. 6. American literature—
    20th century. I. Baer, Barbara L., ed. II. Jennings, Maureen Anne, ed.

    PS571.C2S25 1998   810.8'09287'097941509049
                            QBI97-1531

Cover art by Marylu Downing
Cover design by William Kinnear
Book layout by Janet Bradlor and Carol Fussell

Saltwater,
Sweetwater

Saltwater, Sweetwater

Table of Contents

Suzanne Lipsett	Night to Day	5
Bonnie Olsen McDonell	No Popsicles	9
Patti Trimble	River	15
Miriam Silver	He Threw Him up to the Sky	17
Lynn Watson	Pinnacle	25
Ginny Stanford	Death in the Cool Evening	27
Robin Rule	The String Creek Saga	33
Judi Bari	Judi Bari in Her Own Words	37
Fionna Perkins	Woodswoman	40
	And What Is Happening	
	Where You Live?	41
Sunlight	View from a Tree	43
Jane Zacharias	Contrabandista	51
Noelle Oxenhandler	The Flavor of Disaster	59
Liza Prunuske	Fog Dance and other poems	65
Robin Beeman	My Phantom Heart	69
Delia Moon	Purple Haze	77
Salli Rasberry	The Coffin Garden	79
Annie Wells	Michele	83
	Rescue	85
Pam Cobb	The Grateful Living	87
Jane Kennedy Stuppin	my man	94

Peg Ellingson	At the Tidepool	97
Bobby Markels	Going to the Where?	105
Joanne Surasky	Light	111
Dee Watt	Love from Scotia	117
Christy Wagner	Bon Ami, Mon Amour	121
Karen Eberhardt Shelton	Cows in the Laguna and other poems	127
Joyce Griffin	The Big Apple Splits	131
Mary Gaffney	Gone to Weed	133
Doris B. Murphy	Goblin, a Love Story	139
Eileen Clegg	Once around the Lake	143
Michele Anna Jordan	Rock Salt and Nails	149
Marianne Ware	Traveling Appetites	153
Glory Leifried	The Congregation	161
Marilyn B. Kinghorn	Walking the Tracks to Graton	167
Marylu Downing	Native	169
J.J. Wilson	Bury My Heart—Where?	177
Susan Swartz	The Portable Mother	181
Suze Pringle Cohan	Wedding	187
Sally Jane Spittles	Mathewing	193
Barbara L. Baer	Venus at Center Forward	195
Linda Noel	Ancestral Strength	203
	Knots	204
Sara Peyton	Weeping Baskets	205
Sarah Flowers	Ground Heat	213
Nancy Kay Webb	Predators and Pagans	215
Simone Wilson	Bridges	219
Maureen Anne Jennings	Waking the Dead	227
Susan Bono	In Passing	235
The Authors		240
The Artists and Photographers		245
Acknowledgments		247

Introduction

We found the theme for *Saltwater, Sweetwater,* writing about our lives on California's North Coast, in the winter months of 1997. Author Suzanne Lipsett had recently died and environmental activist Judi Bari was gravely ill with inoperable cancer. The dozen women who had put together a first collection of writing, *Cartwheels on the Faultline,* retreated to the North Coast to envision another book.

Losing Suzanne Lipsett and Judi Bari so young to breast cancer devastated and frightened all of us. Whether or not we knew them personally, their courageous lives and deaths touched everyone who read about them. Suzanne and Judi died at the most creative time in their lives, with major work ahead and young children who still needed them. Suzanne wrote and worked as an editor through a decade of illness. The bomb that had blown up under Judi Bari's car seat had crippled but not stopped her; she organized rallies, protested, wrote, and sang through pain. To hold Suzanne and Judi in our minds longer, to honor them, we would write about the places they loved, from what Suzanne called the Sonoma savannas, to the rugged beauty and ancient forests of the North Coast. These places gave Suzanne and Judi their inspiration and purpose.

Our first collection, *Cartwheels on the Faultline,* had bubbled up with a fountain of ideas. Unlimited, unrestrained by a theme, the book could barely contain the voices of twenty-seven Sonoma County women writing about anything and everything we wanted to say. By contrast, *Saltwater, Sweetwater* has had a direction from the start and has grown like a river, deepening as it gathered in tributaries.

Early on, Maureen Jennings and I recognized a curious unity running through many of the manuscripts we received. All the writers understood that we were dedicating the book to Suzanne and Judi and that every piece had to touch on or be about place. The writings were all regionally connected, but beyond that, a remarkable number of them were also about ghosts, about bridging the worlds of life and death. Many stories and memoirs and poems, even the funny ones, seemed haunted, as if resisting separation and loss. As we opened envelopes with manuscripts tucked inside, we wondered if we were calling to phantoms. Or were they calling us?

Suzanne Lipsett knew that her last novel, *Remember Me,* was her finest, and the critics acclaimed it. She next published a memoir, *Surviving a Writer's Life,* that blended her evolution as an artist with an exploration of the difficulties that loving words and making a living as an editor had always presented. Suzanne's husband, Tom Rider, has given us one of the essays from a book she was completing before she died. Suzanne never stopped writing her own work or editing books for others. She connected many friends in Sonoma County who cared about literature.

Judi Bari came to Mendocino County from the East in the late 1970s, fell in love with redwoods, and became the heart and the voice calling us to save the Headwaters Forest and all the old-growth groves on the North Coast. At Judi's memorial, people wore tee-shirts that said, "Don't Mourn. Organize!" Fionna Perkins, a long-time peace activist and environmentalist from Gualala, cautioned me, "Don't make too much of Judi's death, focus on her life. She was not a martyr but a hero." We are donating part of the profits from our book to the Environmental Protection Information Center dedicated to preserving Headwaters Forests and the old-growth groves surrounding it.

As we had done for *Cartwheels,* women in small groups met to read, encourage, question, and criticize each other's manuscripts. An editorial board considered all submissions in a "blind reading," then made the selections together. Maureen and I edited the work. Marylu Downing painted the woman on the cover. She asked local artists for images of women, of forests and rivers, of sunny hillsides, and resting places like the

Druids Cemetery in Occidental, where, last year, Nancy Farah, another beloved woman who died of cancer in her forties, was laid to rest.

We chose our title when we saw how many of us were considering the sweet rivers of life flowing out to the sea. We hope that our readers will find and lose themselves in our stories about the places to which we are giving a writer's reality, the places we love and want to preserve, our places along California's North Coast.

Barbara L. Baer   1997

Night to Day

Suzanne Lipsett

Most people, I think, would begin with the birds. The soft
light filters in through the swaying white curtain, dawn yields
to morning, I open my eyes without moving at all, lying still
—Tom already up and gone—and listen to the birds.

That's partly how it is this morning of tentative health, soft
health, after the battering I've taken, but not completely. Most
of the sounds of morning are dominated by the cows.

They are anomalies, these cows in the side pasture behind
my window. Far from placid and quiet, they are continuously
working each other up into hysterical bellowing fits. One
begins, honking through the trees and grasses like a noisemaker
trumpet at a sporting event. After a string of repetitions—
honk, honk, honk—a hint of surprise, then outrage, tinges the
sounds, and then another restless bovine picks up the cry:
hanukkah, hanukkah, hanukkahhh. I suppose that technically
it is more a bellow than the trumpeting of a wind instrument,
but "bellow" fails to convey the ascension up the scales. These
become urgent sounds, echoed all around the pasture, with an
undertone of lows as a kind of bass line.

Through years of nights and mornings I have listened to
the cows, and consider the explanation for their racket to be
nothing more exotic than gross laziness. Down here by the
house and under the swaying oaks, bay laurels, and buckeye
trees, the cows cluster at the dry creek bed waiting and waiting
for water. In winter, yes, the creek bed fills, and the ribbons of
water add their burblings to the mass of interwoven sounds.
But not now, not in May. There's been no water in Blue Jay
Creek for months, and winter is so far in the future as to be
unimaginable. Granted, the pond for drinking is far away—

across the flat back pasture that spreads behind our house and over the first hump of yellowing hills. But isn't it merely the work of cows to plod heavily through the grass, feeding, grinding, digesting in those famous swaying stomachs, and eventually reaching the pond where they can drink?

These lazy cows: how I appreciate their loud complaints this morning. Finally, something to think about that has nothing to do with, is far outside, my body.

I cannot lie: the subject is cancer. Overworked, overdone, oversentimentalized, overused as a metaphor for mortality in an era that secretly considers death to be a curable disease. I am so self-conscious about writing of cancer—my cancer, another phrase that gags me—that I actually feel a blush (me? blush?) when I see these very words on my computer screen. I'm alone in the house, but will somebody suddenly appear by chance and see that I'm writing about It? Barring one highly light-handed reference in a book, I have avoided writing about cancer as assiduously as I would about going to the bathroom. Wary, chary, fearful of reinforcing a reality that can, if forgotten, become ephemeral for long, blessed periods of time. I am accustomed to stepping around the horror that has resided within my body for nearly ten years. Ten years of intermittent crisis, each more fearsome than the ones before. No one would blame me, I know, for galloping away whenever I can. Everyone would understand the soothing consolation of denial.

This time, though, I cannot shake it. I am stunned at the profundity of what I've just gone through. It began a couple of months ago with a growing awareness of encroachment—that perhaps owing to the Africa-like landscape we live in, the beautiful Sonoma savanna—I can only compare to the relentless trudge of a column of army ants. Remember the movie? Was it *Elephant?* The ants came through the countryside like a train through the grass, following the contours of all it encountered: up over a gully, down a hillside, across a wash, through a village, over a cow, rounding up over an elephant, and then—terrible!—onto a man. It reduced everything to nothing, or to bone. It, a monstrous singular composed of millions and millions of entities, devoured everything in its path.

A perfect symbol of cancer. Inexorable. Unstoppable. Utterly, neutrally natural.

Chemotherapy was unavoidable, inevitable, and my body's response to it more awful than I had anticipated over a decade of phobia. It's funny, almost a practical joke, that the administering of the chemical is almost pleasant—a comfortable peridontist's type chair, a VCR if you remember to bring videos (I watched *Clueless*—perfect!), and plenty of good conversation with the nurses and a social worker who slowly revealed her deep Zen learnings to me. Then followed days of exhilaration, during which I felt high at having weathered something I'd feared for so long—one can allow oneself to seem a little heroic for a second. Ha, ha, Ms. Triumphant. Not so fast. Three good days, and you're *down*.

I retreated into a cellar I didn't know I had. There are dreams in which you suddenly discover rooms to your house that you hadn't ever seen. For me, with the ants on the trudge, chewing toward me, I found a cellar. My husband Tom came with me, and through this dark Dostoevskian cavern blew gales of pain and maniacal distress as cruel and indifferent to our presence as a cosmic storm one might imagine sweeping and howling through space. Tom hovered, and I guttered, like a candle flame dashed sideways and at risk of sizzling out in its own little pool of wax.

So I discover, with apologies to the hopeful New Age enthusiasts who treasure wholeness so, that, for me at any rate, self and body are quite separate, and in the presence of even a thumb's weight of nature's power, the self is a shaky little spark so close to going out that there is hardly a dividing line at all.

Clearly, I did not expire. In all sensibleness, I must admit I came not remotely close. Yet with Tom cupping the flame, blowing on it—love becomes air, becomes action—still I felt the breath of that terrible storm. Momentarily, begging for escape, I could have rushed into it.

This morning, though, I awoke not to my own internal troubles but to the cows' commotion. True, I am a little petulant with thirst and irritation, but the storm has blown away. Inside my body, which is shaky and weak, my being stands like a flame in a still room: erect, barely moving, translucent to yellow to blue. A hawk cuts across my window and I wish, as I always wish, I could hear the shuddering of air through its feathers. A jay squawks, and little twitters close and far dot the air outside my window. Breeze through the oak trees rattles their leaves, air fingers furrow the grasses. All this holds my attention, and I jump with a startle at a sudden electronic shriek: the telephone, and it is Tom, the love of my life, hovering once more in my ear.

No Popsicles

Bonnie Olsen McDonell

The flood of 1995 ripped the gas tank from my mother's yard, wrecked the furnace, and filled her lot with debris from other people's lives: flowered underwear hanging like a flag from a widow-maker branch on a redwood, chew toys and a paddle, painted brown by silt, rammed through the porch lattice by the force of the Russian River.

The day before the flood we'd driven out to the summer house to raise Mom's furniture, and watched in amazement as the river sucked up the bank toward the house, its brown meniscus bulging with branches and tires. Propane tanks shot towards Jenner like giant silver suppositories.

But now, it's June, and back to the languid green stream I've stroked since childhood. We're picnicking on Monte Rio Beach, a mile east of the summer house, bathed in sunscreen. My kids have been splashing around since morning. Finally, sluggish from lunch, they doze at my mother's feet and I risk a solitary dip.

I swim to the far side of the river, dodging a novice canoeist, and find footing on huge boulders submerged in front of the Highland Dell Hotel. I try to imagine the other river here, that massive brown bag of a river, slurping up roads and houses and the air above my head.

I look back at the beach, automatically scanning for a faded green and orange Sea-and-Ski umbrella. I hear Carly before I see the kids. A sinus-clearing scream, followed by "Mama!" She's heading for the water. My mother, her Nana, follows stiffly, in the yellow and black swimsuit she has had since I was ten.

I start back, amazed again at the pleasure of swimming in the old river, soft current tugging briefly at my feet, as I breaststroke through the channel. The older kids are battling, rolling around on the beach blanket like two angry puppies. My mother holds Carly's hand. Her back is to me but her voice drifts across the shimmering surface of the water. "Can't you control yourselves? No popsicles at three o'clock if you keep that up!" A threat I remember. Nana and the kids will not endure till three. We've flung skippers, hunted pollywogs, and swum our fingertips to pale raisins.

I grab my faded beach towel. "What do you say we rent a canoe, Mom? Check your property." Big chunks of her river bank had cracked away and fallen into the water like dirt bergs in years past, and the path to the river had collapsed.

She sighs, turning around slowly, staggering slightly in her compressed thongs. "I'd like that." She lowers herself into a sandchair. "I haven't gotten a good look since before your father died." She pours herself some ice tea. "Sylvia, your children exhaust me."

"Me, too," I reply. Mara has amassed a pile of bait shells, Scott, a pile of skippers. They eye each others' stashes jealously, ready for another tussle.

Nana reaches for her big black purse. Number fifty or so in a line of big, black purses. "Here's the money."

I push her hand away. "My treat, Mom. Scott, Mara, let's rent a canoe."

Carly throws her bucket at the ground, stomping her fat little feet on the hot rocks, "I want to come! I want to come!"

The children grab my hands and we wend our way through a patchwork of beach blankets to the rental stand. Nana gets five minutes of peace.

I drag a dusty Grumman canoe towards the water and toss in the plastic paddles. Scott cinches up his lifejacket, eyes wide. "Do these tip over?"

"Only if you fool around." I brush off the sandy silver floor of the boat, waiting for my mother to hide her wallet and car keys, hike down the beach, and grab a paddle. "Once your daddy and I were in a canoe race. We'd won the race for the past two years and had to defend our title. That spring Daddy had really gotten into rowing. He kept telling me to 'put your body into your stroke, Sylvia.' I did. I leaned into my stroke like he said, he leaned into his on the same side, and over we went!"

"Did you win the race?" Scotty throws a rock into the shady water under the bridge.

"No, but we got the biggest laugh." I run my hand through his bristle-thick hair.

Scott's next rock cracks against the bridge support. "Don't put your body into it today, Mommy."

We tighten the girls' lifejackets and board, Mom in her post-cataract, Ray Charles sunglasses, then Scott, Mara, and Carly. I heave us into deeper water, hop in behind Carly, and we head downstream. Once we are beyond the bridge I plan to drag the canoe through the shallows and let the kids paddle. We ease under the bridge, throwing echoes against the shady stanchions. Back in sunlight, we pass a shoal.

Suddenly an eddy swings the boat around in an arc and plunges us into a wall of willows. Carly's polka-dot hat blows into the water. A low moan escapes from Scott. "I'm scared, Mommy. We're going to tip over."

"Quiet," I tell him. "We'll be fine." I backpaddle madly to punch through the eddy. We re-enter the main body of the river heading downstream.

There are no shallows.

A cold bar of fear stiffens my shoulders. The river is broader than I've ever seen it here. It is dark-green deep and as wide as a lake.

Gusts of wind force us sideways toward the sour willow-scented bank. Twenty feet above us a red-checkered tablecloth snaps against a tree.

There are no other vessels in sight.

Scott's voice shakes. "Mommy, I want to go home." Mara finger paints in the mud film on the floor of the canoe. Carly shifts her pink and orange striped bottom over the midseam.

"Where's Nana's house? Where's my hat?"

"Nana's house is coming up faster than you think. Don't move around." I concentrate on keeping us straight, fighting the afternoon gusts blowing up from Jenner. The wide river abruptly narrows into a shoot and we surge downstream, my paddle a rudder. Familiar houses dart past us. A heron croaks from a lopsided dock, now upstream.

The metal bar shifts to my gut. How were we going to get back? A seventy-two-year-old woman, three children under eight, and me, the idiot. "Well, your house is zooming right up, Mom. Why don't we pull into shore and look for a minute?"

We let the wind thrust the bow to the far side of the channel. I seize a pair of branches, clenching the seat with my calves. Mom gazes across the river, looking for land loss, studying her summerhouse, so still and inviting beneath the redwoods. I ache for the lost stairs, the path, the dock, but face instead a bulwark of willows and poison oak.

I flash on the memory of Mom and Dad sitting on the dock, reading short stories to each other in the late afternoon, the hills of Cazadero a golden silhouette to the west. I think of my father, what he would do. He patiently taught me to row and paddle and drive. Go on if you have to, he'd say. He would be calm. His dentures would click with anxiety but he would otherwise appear calm.

"So, Mom, if we can't get back up, we'll float down to Villa Grande Beach, use a phone. You guys ready?"

Scott turns, his eyes thick with tears. "Are we gonna die, Mom?"

"No," I say reassuringly, but as I try to orient the canoe upstream I notice that Villa Grande Beach is submerged.

Carly smiles, her thick blond baby curls flashing as she turns. "Can I paddle now?"

I'm driving my strokes into the water. We're facing upstream. Sweat pours sunscreen into my eyes. "No way, honey," I pant.

Her face folds into misery. "But I want to. I want to," she wails. "I want to get my hat."

The wind pushes us up and the current pulls us back. "Hush," I command her. "Remember those popsicles."

With constant strokes we move inches. Finally we pass a neighbor's house.

"But I want to get into your lap." Carly begins to stand; the canoe jiggles.

Scott's scream is guttural. "We're gonna drown!"

"We're okay. Stay calm. It helps me paddle," I force a smile up and the nausea down. Scott huddles into himself.

Mara gazes at the birds flying over. "Hawks, Mom." I don't tell her they are buzzards.

We pass another house. I heave my paddle into the water, harder, harder.

My mother raises her paddle to rest. We stop moving. Her sun-freckled shoulders rise and fall. I am grateful that she quit smoking. We start to slide downstream, pulled by the invisible arms of the current.

"Nana, deep strokes on the left. Let's keep going." We pass a few more houses. My heart jackhammers against my chest. I lean in.

"Don't put your body into it! Don't!" Scott bangs the metal for emphasis.

"Okay," I whisper. My arms ache. My mother's knees are shaking, planted hard into the hull. She paddles on, too winded to speak.

"I can see the bridge," Mara offers, nodding to herself. We press on, grunting with our desperate strokes. Suddenly we're out of the shoot. My mother lifts up her paddle and lays it across her knees. I guide us across the wide, deep expanse of unexpected lake and we catch the tail of Monte Rio Beach.

"Look!" Mara cries. "There goes Carly's hat." We watch the dotted cap bob across the lake, enter the shoot, and get sucked under, snatched by the swift hand of the river.

"Bye, bye," says Carly.

Steadying the boat with my foot, I lift the children out to the welcome hot rocks then lend a trembling arm to my mother.

"Don't ever do that again!" she snarls, her face florid, creeks of sweat pouring down her neck.

River

Patti Trimble

It's about little circles of breathing
color of blue in a square foot of sky
arc of tree branch
shameless face of moon
turn of your hand in conversation
the down time each month
a sudden impulse to kiss
and my eye judging the distance
from here to there
and back again.

He Threw Him up to the Sky

Miriam Silver

Come with me to the ocean.

Come let me show you the special green the Pacific turns. A lazy, languorous green. Come hear the sound, the softness, the muting, the blending of the edges, the extraordinary calm when the muscular water stretches like a mother cougar after her babies have gone to sleep.

Yeah, right. I could talk this way to my father. Right. Like he would listen. Like here is a man who now spends half his conversation on the weather, whatever the season. It's so hot. It's so cold. Crazy snowstorm. Temperatures close to ninety. Humidity won't quit. Yes, the air conditioner works. No, I haven't gone outside. It's miserable out there.

Will he hear the waves? He did once.

It's my own little miracle I am working on. I have this idea. That if my father comes out here to live, I can teach him to hear and to see new things. Quite a task at eighty. Or forty-five even.

When I was little, I'd run to his lap, tuck myself into his arms, and get ready for the show. Books were performances. Every character got a voice. His Rapunzel was sweet and high-pitched. She talked so rapidly I often missed it. But it didn't matter because each character also had enormous gestures. My father's witch grabbed the nearest towel, threw it on his head, and skulked around my bed, jumping on and off to make his point. I loved every minute of it.

On the last visit back East, my four-year-old son sat on that same lap. Thinner legs, less hair, thicker glasses. I was surprised when my father seemed to gather energy as he acted out *Green Eggs and Ham.* Toby squawked and screamed and laughed, fell sideways off the couch, and scrambled back onto my father's lap.

A few days later, Toby and I are back home. My father calls.
To tell me how much he misses us.

"I couldn't wait every morning until Toby opened the door
and came in. He took my life and threw it up to the sky."

My mother died when I was fifteen. For a while, it was just
Dad and me. Later, it was just him. And that's been okay until
recently when a bout of pneumonia threw him over the edge of
elderly into frail. He's given up his car, more easily than I
expected. I had suggested it on our last visit. We were walking
in a park, the one down the street from our old house. It was
East Coast October, turning gradually into autumn, warm then
cool, patchy green grass, yellow leaves, clean sky. At home in
Sonoma County, it was brash heat and light, what I once
thought of as dry brittle weeds but had finally come to see as
great glistening stalks. October is lovely just about everywhere.
But this was fall where I grew up, a fresh and new time. Even as
a kid, I thought, you often get the clearest view as the year was
coming to its end.

"I've never walked here," my father said as we watched
Toby throw rocks into the creek.

"I used to come here all the time."

"You did? I didn't know that. What for?"

I thought about seeing my mother's wheelchair for the first
time and then climbing onto my bike, slamming it into third
gear to get to the top of the hill, and zooming down as fast as I
could, wet eyes, notebook shoved into my pants at the back. I'd
throw down my bike under a tree, sit up against it, and write
hard and fast, while I talked out loud until I could stop crying.

"Oh, I used to come here to write."

"How old were you?"

"Ten, eleven. Until I could drive."

He squinted in the afternoon glare. He looked out at the
creek. He didn't look back at me.

"I didn't know that," he said again.

"Dad, can we talk about the car now?"

"What's to talk about? How can I get around? I don't drive
it very far. To the grocery. Maybe to pick up some shirts. How
else would I get there? It's too far to walk. How would I get to
the doctor?"

"Dad, there are cabs, and drivers, and people to help you."

"I admit, I've been thinking about it. Maybe I could get a college kid to give me rides. I don't like the car anymore. But I don't know what I'd do without it."

He volunteered the other stuff. The accidents.

"Your aunt was okay. Just hit the side of her arm. I misjudged the turn. I banged up that other car good, though. Didn't get mine fixed. Costs too much. Guess how much I pay in insurance?"

I guessed on the high side. "Fifteen hundred dollars."

"Five thousand," he said.

A couple of weeks after our talk, he sells his car to a guy who works in his building. Says he got $2,000 and seems pretty happy about that.

"I'm making friends with the cab drivers. Yeah, they all know me. Seems like a lot of money just to go get a paper, though."

So I have this idea. Crazy, maybe, but why not? Why not be together again? Toby would love it. Dad'd love it. And me, well, it's not going to be just me again for a long time anyway. What I want to do is pack him up and bring him here to Sebastopol. I remember when he helped me look for my house, and just about died when he saw the price of this small, three-bedroom bungalow on the edge of a hillside vineyard. Now, he whistles at the memory of it.

"That is some place. I love that house," he says during one of our nightly phone conversations. "Nice little town. God, I wish I could live there."

"Why can't you?"

This to a man who used to travel 3,000 miles to visit but stay only two nights, three days, tops. He'd always preface with, "Can't overstay your welcome. Gotta get home. Three days is plenty."

But now his longing is palpable.

A Thanksgiving in the '70s was the first time he visited here. I wanted it to be perfect. Thanks to a drought, it almost was. We wore only cotton sweaters when we drank coffee outside on the deck. We walked to the corner for a paper. Oh, the things he noticed.

"Unbelievable. Look at all these cars. Not a speck of dirt on them. Even the white ones. This is living," he had said.

I am reminding him of the Thanksgiving meal on the beach with my new friends. Even a few seals lounging on the rocks. Hollywood couldn't have done it better.

"Yep. No forgetting that," he says. "Throwing a ball, on the beach, in the middle of November for God's sake. What was the name of that town?"

"Jenner."

"Yeah, Jenner. Now that was living."

Okay, almost, I almost have him. But no. He switches.

"You and Toby are so damned far away. And I can't leave your mother."

"Dad, she's gone."

Sometimes he just loses track. No one to take care of or to help him tell the black socks from the navy blues. Looks like he stopped wearing them anyway. Too hard to get them right. I can picture exactly what he's doing as we talk. He's sitting still in his beige leather easy chair, the arms gray from newspapers, the material on the headrest wearing thin. He fingers the pencils on his desk. He stares at an old picture of my mother in her engagement dress, crepe draped to the floor, tulip neckline, full red lips, dark hair shaping her face. Benny Goodman. The Swing. After the War.

"Your mother was something. Just a ball of fire. When I came back from Germany, that other one was waiting for me. But it turned out, your mother was too. I forgot all about that other girl. Your mother had written all those letters. I always got one. And when I came home, she grew up. Three years. No longer that skinny little thing. You should have seen her then."

I always wanted to see her then. I wanted to be them then. But, mine would never be as good as theirs. That's probably why it's just me and Toby. When I was growing up, sometimes I felt my head was lost in the '40s, steeped in their postwar euphoria, platform heels, lipstick smiles, thin mustaches. I thought she was a beautiful lady. I'd drag her wedding gown out of her cedar closet, and try it on over my dungarees. My waist was too big even at twelve. Torn white lace.

Old story. Before the War. The War. After the War. When

Your Mother Got Sick. The four parts of my father's life.

I have to help him have one more.

"Dad, you could live with us. There's nothing there anymore."

I remember when we were saying goodbye at a corner in New York twenty years ago. We had just finished lunch, and he was on his way to the train station to go home. I told him I was quitting school and leaving for California. He didn't seem surprised.

"What will you do?"

"Get a job until I can get into school out there."

"For God's sake, you can't just go, and leave everything, and do that. You can't just go."

"Dad…"

He stopped looking at me. He stared out at the street, at a woman getting out of a cab. And then back at me.

"Of course you can. Of course you can just go. I always wanted to go there. Now maybe I'll get there someday."

He hugged me tightly, turned away, and threw up his arm to hail a cab. It stopped faster than either of us expected. That was our first goodbye.

He's been sending lots of packages lately. He's cleaning things, throwing out, organizing. This last box is light, and filled with styrofoam balls. A crumpled piece of paper torn from an old notebook. Familiar scribbles, short, sweet, to the point. "These are all that are left in quasi-usability. What the H! Love Dad."

Inside are four old dolls, souvenirs from his mother's trips—one dressed in Dutch garb, another Spanish. A little Chinese girl, two braids, red silk pajamas, shoes missing. A black feather drops out. Toby picks it up and blows on it.

"Make a wish, Mama."

Toby's probably wishing the box had been filled with tractors. I don't know what to do with these dolls. I don't think they're worth anything. But my father probably does. He thinks a lot of the stuff he is finding is worth something.

One visit, dumb and twenty-four years old, I had flown back to New York where I stayed for a few days before taking the train to Philadelphia. I let Dad know I'd meet him at home. It was one of those awful hot summer days, sweltering humid city, no air, no space. I hadn't eaten much, and was carrying an overloaded backpack, stuffed with copper pans I'd picked up at a flea market. The heat, the exhaustion, and the empty stomach caught up with me. On the subway, I felt warm, and dizzy. I got off before my stop, sat on the ground, and leaned against a pillar until the nausea subsided. I was so scared I thought I'd faint right there, and be left to die. I managed to get to the train station, dragged myself to a phone booth, and called my father to ask him to meet me on the other end in Philadelphia. Still woozy, I could hardly stop from gagging on the phone. I couldn't hide it. And, as always, he knew I'd overdone it.

"Wait there. I'll come pick you up."

"My train leaves in just a minute or two. Don't worry."

"Eat something."

I was barely awake when I heard the conductor yell, "Next stop, Thirtieth Street." I stepped onto the platform and saw my father running toward me. He grabbed my backpack, and stuck a cold can of ginger ale in my hand.

"Here. Drink this. I got a corned beef sandwich in the bag. You gotta' eat something."

He has met me so many times, it's time for me to meet him.

Uncharacteristically, he makes the call.

"Why not. I mean why the hell not? But I'm getting my own place. Right away. I'm not going to crowd you and Toby."

I talk to his doctor who issues vague instructions on what to do if his memory gets worse.

My aunt gets him packed. She doesn't seem to believe it's really happening.

"I know you are very independent. You have always been that way. But, are you sure this is right?" she asks.

I'm sure. However odd the configuration, this is my family. Me, Dad, and Toby.

I find an easy chair at a garage sale down the street. I buy a new lamp. A twin bed, new and all his own. Toby helps me paint a bookshelf that we decorate with two pictures, one of my father's young mother reading in a wicker rocking chair, and the other of him and Toby naming trees as they walked in the park. There's a tape player and two tapes, *Frank Sinatra, the Capitol Years* and *Benny Goodman's Hits of 1948.*

It is one of those warm October days, but Toby insists on wearing the red wool 49ers cap my father sent him when he was born. We arrive at the United gate about an hour earlier than we need to.

We wait until about thirty-five million people get off the plane. It's all I can do to stop Toby from running through the doors when my father comes walking out, white cardigan buttoned wrong, sneakers, no socks, trenchcoat balled up under his arm.

Toby runs over and thrusts the warm can of Coke into his hand, and crawls up his legs. I watch my father bend, and lift Toby with a strength I have not seen in a long time.

"Come with us, Dad, to the ocean."

Pinnacle

Lynn Watson

She was a beach he'd wanted to walk down all his life.
When he found her, there was no day fee at the gate.
The proponents of Free-the-Sonoma-Coast had been
victorious. *The Press Democrat* ran a front page story
in their weekend section, promoting the easy half-mile
walk down to the water. Now everyone and his brother
would be parking at the top of the hill, hauling lawn chairs
and coolers. It was still February, and freezing temperatures
were on his side. A three-dollar entry fee was being imposed
as of March. How he hated crowds. He slipped down the wet,
muddy path, leaving his dog Rex back at the house. Today
he wanted her all to himself. It was a foggy Tuesday and no
other footprints marred the sand. She was white, delicate,
glorious. How he loved the blue of her eyes, smiling only
for him. Today she brought two baby sand dollars as a token.
He picked them up, feeling a sudden warmth in his hand.
He looked back up the trail for Dieter and his dog Shanti
whose pictures had appeared in the paper. No, they
wouldn't come today. He had her all to himself.

Death in the Cool Evening

Ginny Stanford

I've always called it love at first sight. What I mean is a compelling visceral attraction that overpowers competing instincts, any tendency to caution or reason. When Frank said hello I fell in love with his voice. By the end of that day, I was sure I loved everything he had been, was then, would ever be. He was wildly enthusiastic about my painting—there's nothing like being understood. In the weeks that followed I read from his manuscripts and made drawings based on the poems. He bought me notebooks and different kinds of pens to try out. He said, Paint an old man sitting by a coffin waving at the moon; a fat lady shelling peas and a centaur behind her; a blind Gypsy holding a conch shell. Paint a white horse breaking away from a funeral hearse; a scarecrow wearing a kimono. Paint smoke rings.

I'd never heard anything like it.

Back then I was sure of many things. I believed Frank and I would always be together, and that time would only bring us more of what we wanted, as if the course of our lives had been set to trace an unwavering line upwards toward happiness and achievement.

I have never regretted for one moment leaving the Midwest, although sometimes I miss the farm—our rambling old house with the front porch that wrapped around two sides, the elaborate garden we had, all the land. Sometimes I miss the prairie and its panoramic views of each day's beginning and end. I loved watching that sky. Things are so different here in northern California. Coastal hills, ghosts of old mountain ranges barricade the eastern horizon. I don't see the first giant copper edge of the moon rising out of the earth like I used to, but nothing the Midwest has to offer can compare with the sight of that enormous red crescent sinking into the Pacific in the middle of the night.

Bodega Head is where I go to watch the moon set—November and December are the best months. I've never been scared to take the path on the crest of those high cliffs alone late at night. Perhaps I should be. A buck deer and I met once in the dark; I saw the white smoke coming out of his nostrils before I saw him.

Frank had been the one so at home around water. I never thought I'd end up feeling the same way. Now I can't imagine leaving here. Living on the western edge of this continent, so far away from where I began, is reassuring to me now—the whole country behind me; two mountain ranges, two time zones, and nearly twenty years now lie between me and the hot oppressive summer of his death. I've had plenty of time to go over that Saturday, wonder why I didn't see it coming, parse every sentence I uttered—every word—comb through everything I did but wish I hadn't, and everything I wanted to say but didn't. As if my taking out one part could have changed the outcome.

He died before I had time to finish his portrait. In May he said, "Copy this Gauguin and paint me standing in front of it. Call it *Spirit of the Dead Watching.*" A Tahitian girl is clutching her pillow in fear. Her bed a sumptuous pattern of blue, rose, yellow, and bright orange. A spray of phosphorescent flowers decorates the wall behind her. At the foot of the bed is another woman, hooded, dressed in black. She sits, staring impassively ahead. She is *manao tupapao,* the spirit of the dead watching. I thought it was a great idea. I thought he had the best ideas. Why don't you pose in your kimono, I said.

We buried him barefoot in that kimono. The funeral home said no at first. They insisted he wear a suit and shoes. Claimed it was a state law. Sometime in the weeks after his death I rolled up the canvas and placed it in a corner of my parents' attic where it remains.

"I love you," was the last thing he said to me. He said I love you and I said, "Don't give me that crap."

Saturday evening. June third. He had betrayed me by having

an affair and I had found him out. I was hurt and humiliated and angry enough to put him through a wall. I barely tolerated the hug he tried to give me, my arms stiff at my sides. He tried to kiss me and I turned my head so that his lips only grazed my hair. Then he left. Forever. He left me in a room and shut the door behind him as he left, and he took three steps across a hall into another room and shut another door and shot himself.

In the span of the longest five or six seconds I have ever lived through, Frank fired three shots into his chest. Three pops, three cries. All I had was sound. I couldn't see him; I could only imagine what he was doing in another part of the house. With the sound of the first shot time stopped, changed course and went backwards through the second and third shots, then reconstructed itself into an endless, directionless loop. Before Saturday, June third, time was a straight line. After Saturday, a loop.

I heard a sharp crack, a hard slap, an angry teacher breaking his ruler against a desk. I heard the crack and just as sharp I heard Frank hollering, "Oh"—surprised. I heard him step on a copperhead, get stung by a yellow jacket, smash his thumb with a hammer. I watched him jump into Spider Creek, heard him hit the cold water and yelp from the shock. Pop Oh! Pop Oh! Pop Oh!

After the third cry I knew he was dead. Imagine the wall is telling you a bedtime story. Go to sleep now, it might say. That is how the news was delivered. A quiet voice from somewhere inside me said flatly, It's all over; he's killed himself. I didn't want to move. But the same silent voice was ordering me out. Get out, get out, it kept repeating. Call the police.

I didn't want to look. He's blown his brains out, the voice said. Don't go in there. Save the memory.

Death had changed his eyes from hazel to pale porcelain green. I climbed onto the bed where he lay and sat astride his crooked body, amazed at the sight of three small red holes ringing his heart. I put my hands on his chest. While I waited for the police I tried to memorize every detail of his face before I never saw it again. He looked through me, toward a distant place and I tried wishing myself there. This is real, I repeated, working hard to convince myself; this is real this is real.

I spent that night in a Holiday Inn. I was afraid to close my eyes, afraid to dream, afraid to let sleep seal the day and lock it into history. Tomorrow, I thought, he will be irretrievable. Finally, against my will, I slept, and not fitfully as I had expected, but deeply. During that long deep sleep—more like a coma—I didn't dream about Frank. I didn't dream at all. He sent no messages, instructions or last requests, and I felt no trace of our connection.

His funeral was like every funeral—inadequate. Stand up. Sit down. Kneel. Pray. Get used to it. I remember the red missal in my lap. It was a deep lush luminous red. The soles of my black shoes clacked on marble tiles, each step echoing through cavernous silence as I made my way to a pew. But what I remember most clearly is Frank's casket—so small and far away—bathed by a pool of dim light. It glowed in the darkness of the church like Sleeping Beauty's glass coffin. I see thick white candles burning in giant brass candlesticks at his head and feet. I think of a clearing in the forest and all the animals in a circle waiting for Sleeping Beauty to open her eyes.

I don't know if the first year was the worst but it was the most singular. Then death was new—every day unique, the first of its kind to be lived without him—and the point was simply to survive. The first year, I couldn't imagine there would be a second one. I anchored myself to painting and stayed busy. It was hard to concentrate on art because I kept expecting someone to burst through the door of the studio and shoot me. I scoured Frank's poems for ideas and ways to stay close to him.

All that year I looked for windows, mirrors, thin fingers of light, something to slip through, some way to find Frank through faith or will on the other side of pain. I dreamed of secret passageways, walls that were really doors opening into life, and Frank vibrant, splendidly alive on the other side of those walls. My nights were full of second chances.

What I saw before me was a desert of time, a white monotony of absence and regret that I could never cross. I imagined him waiting at the end of that long first year with fresh water and a laurel wreath, waving from the finish line to spur me on. "You made it," he might say, "and I'm your reward."

For years I saw him—a gesture, a wave, a blur. His promises were everywhere. *Set me as a seal upon thine heart, as a seal upon thine arm; for love is strong as death.* I thought it was him. I worked hard at forgetting but he stayed with me, beside me, behind me. I felt him waiting, like the fog waits to come in on summer evenings. Just roll in over the hills while I sleep, I told him. You can disappear with the sunrise.

Once I thought I saw him but it was the light hitting my windshield. I thought I saw him but it was a blue jay in a bay tree. I thought I saw him but it was a curtain blowing through a window. I saw a man waiting for the bus and thought it was him. I saw a shadow dancing across a wall and thought it was him. I was expecting him. I had the red carpet out. A black cat jumped down out of a tree and I thought it was him. I heard something like his voice but it belonged to an owl. I thought I saw him but it was smoke from a brush pile. I thought it was him but it was my longing, my regret. Sometimes when the phone rang I imagined he might be calling. I said, I love you too. I said it often in case he might be listening.

I studied the photographs I'd taken, looking for clues, and found the other woman in his face. At the point where she entered our lives I saw lies cross-hatching, shadowing his cheeks, filling in below his eyes with darkness. The smile began fading in and out; it grew less frequent. Finally his jaw became a clenched fist, clamped down tight on honesty, choking it back; his face seemed fossilized. He looked driven, wild, worn out in the last pictures. I decided she had killed him.

During the fifth summer of his death, I opened one of his books and read a poem on the last page and I remembered our life purposefully. To console myself I painted a meadow like the meadow at the farm—prairie hay turning copper in October light, intersecting an eastern sky infiltrated by the beginnings of darkness. I painted my longing as a red silk kimono with its pattern of tiny pink and white gourds, floating above the tall grass. The seventh summer I took off my wedding ring and put it in a pine trunk. The eighth summer I gave all his records to the Santa Rosa Public Library. I couldn't bear to listen to the music of our life. The tenth summer I wore his Saint Francis medal.

I painted his portrait during the thirteenth summer and we

became friends again. On the fourteenth anniversary of his suicide I fired a twenty two revolver at a paper target. It felt a little like murder. Did you feel the pain? I asked. How were you able to keep pulling the trigger? Why didn't you drop the gun? Why did you leave? I hit the bull's eye twice.

Three months later, on August first, I celebrated his birthday for the first time in a long time. Instead of a cake I bought a package of twelve inch red tapers. I collected all the candlesticks in the house and arranged them in a circle on the dining room table and put my bouquet in the center—his favorite flowers, bachelor buttons, mixed with yellow coreopsis and white cosmos, tied with a red ribbon. I'd picked them from the flower bed by the front door. The fog was beginning to roll in and soften the long shadows that fell across my deck. I lit the candles at dusk—fifteen in all—and stepped back to take in the sight. He would get a kick out of this, I thought.

June third comes and goes. I grow older and Frank remains forever twenty-nine. Time has taught me, among other things, that death is persistent and enduring beyond my capacity to imagine it. People still ask me Why? I used to have an answer. Now I say, I don't know.

from
The String Creek Saga

to Judi Bari

Robin Rule
IV

We drive to town, laughing at the wild turkeys
who remind us of gawky teen boys and girls
and we tell funny stories on ourselves
from way back when we were so serious.

You confessed you ironed your long hair and
I crumpled knee socks into my dumb shoes
and we both dreamed bigger than the sixties...

I was gonna be a famous poet
and you, girl, were gonna save the workers.

VIII

Today you told me the bad news. I hold
a paper in my pocket that gives me
what you just lost. How do I face your kids
without guilt, except I have two at home

that love me like there's no tomorrow... What
is this body we carry around, but
a fragile suit of clothes and yes, we've learned

just now on your old front porch, that sometimes,
there is no tomorrow when it's needed most...

IX

You held us and said that we could cry once;
then it's back to the way it was before
you told us you were dying of cancer.
If we couldn't do that, *then get out now…*

You've too much work to do and we can help,
but there's too little time to waste on tears
except for now, as we three stand and hold

each other up. Soon, we will be holding
everything up for you but your spirit…

XIII

Standing on the porch, Tanya and I hear
big whoosh of raven's wings; look up into
the blue bowl sky as bird circles the cabin,
wings beating the air in time to heartbeat.

This grocery list and that message from town:
a litany of chores that pushes back
the nightmare we see in broad daylight.

Radio-woman slumbers and dreams
she's flying over a grove of unmarked trees.

XVIII

Sitting by her bed, as she sleeps drugged
yet fitful to creak and crack of fire
burning down to ash, I watch her breasts rise
and fall like a rhetoric I could listen

to forever…The politics of love
will go on, but as she shudders
in light sleep, I hate the pain-filled nightmare

she journeys through, alone. There is nothing
we can do, but feed dog, split wood, cook food, love.

XXIII

We walk to door to pay our last respects;
give last kiss, tangle fingers in her hair…
Alicia, all hot tears, holds me and points
to the ancient pine twenty feet away:

She's sitting right there, she says with big eyes.
I go home to the dog who whimpers and yips,
following Judi all over the valley…

I laugh, cry, recite Kaddish for women;
change the words to encompass the whole world.

XXIV

So, yeah, it's no use crying for the moon
when she's hanging here in the winter sky
like a fat dime. And no use calling
that local number scrawled on my wall

by the door. No one home…I keep forgetting…
What's it going to take? All these memories
of summer barbecues, long drives to Carlotta…

Your face invades my now-time like yesterday;
your dog at my feet, seed catalogs in my hands.

Judi Bari in Her Own Words

Excerpts from *Timber Wars*

Selecting these passages, Fionna Perkins writes, "To let Judi Bari's pen sketch her own portrait, I used her book, Timber Wars, *as I would a box of fabrics in making a quilt, lifting out bits and pieces of varying size, color, and texture. I used her words as I saw her, a small, audacious woman of great courage with a vision as big as the Earth she loved."*

I hardly wrote anything before the bombing…I put out leaflets and stuff, but mostly I was too busy doing the actions to write about them…Now that I can no longer hike through the woods or throw my body in front of bulldozers, I've become a much more prolific writer….

I used to build yuppie houses out of that old-growth redwood…the best job I could get to support two kids…I was a full-time carpenter…I'm tired of apologizing for my labor background. That's who I am. I was a union organizer for longer than I was an Earth First!er….

One hundred forty years ago the county I live in was primeval redwood forest…impossible to live in the redwood region of Northern California without being profoundly affected by the destruction of this once magnificent ecosystem….

Miles and miles of clearcuts…beelines of log trucks fill our roads, heading to the sawmills with loads ranging from 1,000-year-old redwoods, one tree trunk filling an entire logging truck, to six-inch diameter baby trees that are chipped for pulp…Clearcuts, mudslides, devastation where the forest used to grow….

So it is not surprising that I, a lifetime activist, would become an environmentalist…What is surprising is that I, a feminist, single mother and blue-collar worker, would end up in Earth First!, a "no compromise" direct action group with the reputation of being macho, beer-drinking eco-dudes…the only ones willing to put their bodies in front of the bulldozers and chainsaws to save the trees. They were also funny, irreverent, and they played music.…

Little did I know that by combining the more feminine elements of collectivism and nonviolence with the spunk and outrageousness of Earth First!, we would spark a mass movement.…

After the bombing, it was the women who rose to take my place. Redwood Summer was the feminization of Earth First!, with three-quarters of the leadership made up of women…women holding the base camp together…women holding the actions together…The attorney team is women.…

John Muir once said, "Tug on anything in nature and you find it is connected to everything else."

Now they're fighting to take twenty-year-old baby third-growth trees…biologically they mean the difference between whether the forest can ever recover, or whether it will end up converted to vineyards, subdivisions, or desert.…

So what we are seeing here is a changing of the climate, a drying up of the land. And we are seeing the greenhouse effect kicking in.…

We need to build a society that is not based on the exploitation of Earth at all—a society whose goal is to achieve a stable state with nature for the benefit of all species.…

This is the second assassination attempt on me in ten months, and that's pretty scary…I got run off the road by a logging truck…rammed me without hitting his brakes…a horrible, violent impact, and my car sailed through the air and crashed.…

I reached deep down inside myself and found the courage to go on. It wasn't easy. It took me about a month to make the decision.…

Some of my earliest political experiences were of twenty-year-old national guardsmen beating my eighteen-year-old nonviolent friends senseless.…

And then this year, immediately preceding this bomb blast, I was subjected to a very frightening death threat campaign…I tried to ignore the death threats, but it was getting hard to concentrate. I was scared for my children. I considered going underground.…

Our past actions in the redwood region had drawn no more than 150 participants. But 3,000 people came to Redwood Summer, blocking logging operations and marching through timber towns in demonstrations reminiscent of those against racism in the South. And despite incredible tension and provocation, and despite the grave violence done to me, Earth First! maintained both our presence and our nonviolence throughout the summer....

I knew it was a bomb the second it exploded. I felt it rip through me with a force more powerful and terrible than anything I could imagine. It blew right through my car seat, shattering my pelvis, crushing my lower backbone, and leaving me instantly paralyzed.

I couldn't feel my legs...didn't know such pain existed. I felt the life force draining from me...knew I was dying...tried to think of my children's faces to find a reason to stay alive...the pain was too great, and I couldn't picture them. I wanted to die. I begged the paramedics to put me out....

Three hours after the bombing, I was placed under arrest while still in surgery, charged with transporting the bomb that nearly took my life...

I have a twenty-year history as a nonviolent organizer, and I didn't suddenly turn into a bomb thrower. And I'm certainly not stupid enough to put a bomb under my own car seat and blow myself up....

This huge outpouring from people I know and people I don't know has really been what has sustained me...When I wanted to give up, people wouldn't let me give up, and I don't know how I can express my appreciation for that....

I recently attended a workshop in Tennessee on violence and harassment in the environmental movement...As we each told our tale, I was struck by the fact that the most serious acts of violence had been done to women...the hatred of the feminine...the hatred of life...has helped bring about the destruction of the planet.

And it is the strength of women that can restore the balance we need to survive....

I certainly believe that the Earth comes first...But I don't think you can separate the way our society treats the Earth from the way we treat each other....

I hope I can someday find out who bombed me....

Woodswoman

Fionna Perkins

beware
when women
go into big timber
to hug trees
to sit in trees
to stand between trees
and catskinners
feller-bunchers
D-sixes

using
their bodies
as messages
their lives
as warning

big trees out there
big saws
big angry men

and absent now
the small hand
that beckoned us to risk
and fiddled a tune
to dance to
to sing with
to step out smartly by
on the way to jail
by way of the woods

to save trees
to save ourselves

And What Is Happening Where You Live?

I bring you news from the country.
Two shooting stars,
a Calypso orchid, armies
of Indian warriors,
headdresses feathered burgundy,
patches of sky splashed
on ceanothus, leathery-leafed
salal arrayed in ropes
of pink and white bells,
the huckleberry coral-tipped,
firs fluorescent.

A mateless peacock
on a neighbor's hill
screams these afternoons
and evenings.
'ELP! 'ELP!

Someone's scattered
handfuls of gold coins
into the duff under pines
violets and buttercups.

Seven flop-eared, knobbly-kneed Nubians
arrive, all on the same day.
Two baby does seek homes where
they won't be eaten. Surely,
that silly old bird crying for company
knows the consequences
—more peacocks.

HELP! HELP!

The news from the country
is rain.

Fionna Perkins

View from a Tree

Sunlight

Karin paces the living room, gesturing wildly. "It makes me furious. They're slaughtering the trees. And what can we do about it?" She slumps into a chair. "Write more protest letters nobody reads?"

"Kim told me some people are going to Owl Valley," Heather says. "To try and stop the logging there."

"How?"

"Tree-sitters. Kim's going. And Leslie."

"You mean they're going to *climb* the trees? *Sit* in them? Those redwoods are 200 feet tall!"

Heather nods. "They're doing a training. Tomorrow, I think."

Karin stares out the window at the tree tops emerging from the mist. Sighing, she turns back to Heather, "Are you going?"

"I can't take time off work. Can you?"

"I've got a deadline." She looks out at the trees again. "Maybe I could write the story there."

"If you go, I'll do support. I'll bake cookies to send up to your little platform."

Karin shudders. "Platform? You know I'm scared of heights. Even the orchard ladder."

In the darkness of the forest, Karin stumbles down the steep slope with the other protesters. Each stump she trips on, each blackberry thorn that tears her flesh feels like a warning too late to heed. She wants to sing something courageous, all of them together at top volume, but North Lumber security guards might be scouting around.

They stop at the foot of a tree and throw down their gear. Looking up, Mark nods. "This one's good—no branches for eighty, ninety, feet. I'll go up and rig it, then somebody can move in."

Karin watches him ascend the tree, straight up as though climbing the face of a cliff. Easy for him, she thinks, he's done it for years. Jack and the Beanstalk passing through the cloud— with the wicked giant waiting at the top. She reaches for Heather's hand.

One by one, Mark rigs the platforms. Kim and Leslie climb to theirs as Karin watches. And then they come to hers.

Nothing seems real except her fear. Trembling, she stands beneath the redwood, staring at the little platform, suspended— from what? She looks beyond the platform to the branches above it, beyond the branches to the treetop, beyond the tree-top to the sky. Pale light dilutes the darkness. Time to go.

Mark attaches Karin's harness to her waist. "Okay, go on up."

With a deep breath, she puts her foot into the loop. "Focus on the rope...don't look down...." Mark's instructions march through her mind. "Raise the waist jumar...hang there on it...move the leg jumar up...stand on it...." Terror is only a glance, a thought, away, but the task at hand takes total attention. Inches at a time, she moves up the rope.

The platform dangles above her head. How fragile it looks. A deep breath. Another step up. Another. She reaches her desti-nation, pulls herself on. The platform shifts, swinging with her weight. Her heart pounds. Sweat seeps from her cold forehead. On her knees, she clings to the board, clings to the lifeline, her hand frozen around the rope. Then she looks down, reeling from the height.

Heather waves. Mark calls, "Attach your clip to the safety line around the tree. Detach the jumars from your lifeline. Yeah. Now drop down the other end of the rope, and we'll tie on your supplies. Then we gotta get out of here."

They wave goodbye and slip away through the trees, leaving her alone. A hundred feet above the ground.

She hauls up her pack of food and water and, with shaking hands, lashes it to the platform. Carefully, she coils the rope and places it beside her, still clutching the end attached to the tree. This is her lifeline, her link to the ground, her way down whenever the time comes.

Anything else? She consults the checklist in her mind for tasks to keep her fears at bay. The list completed, she considers her book or her journal, but stretching toward them sets the platform swinging. She recoils. What am I going to *do* up here? Can I handle the waiting? With a shiver, she thinks, I don't even know what I'm waiting for.

The roar of chain saws startles her. They're muffled, some distance away. She tries to see where they are, but her view is screened by the other trees, and the direction is disguised by the echo bouncing off the valley walls.

Exhausted, she unrolls her sleeping bag, but the foot hangs over the platform's edge. She curls up, but the space is hardly wide enough. What if the safety line comes unclipped or the lifeline slips out of her hand? What if she tosses in her sleep? The platform barely holds her lying still.

She faces the trunk of the tree that supports her. Huge, solid. It's been here for hundreds of years, she thinks, I should be able to count on it. Lacy branches fan out around it. One brushes her head. Still gripping the rope, Karin reaches up with her other hand to touch the twig, running her fingers through its needles as it runs its needles through her hair. The touch gives her courage and she dares to close her eyes.

A wind comes up and rocks her bed, evoking the grim nursery tune which runs uninvited through her mind.

> Rock a bye baby
> On the tree top,
> When the wind blows
> The cradle will rock,
> When the wind stops
> I'll take to the sky,
> And that is the way
> I'll learn how to fly.

She sings it over and over until she falls asleep, held in the strength of the mother tree.

Voices from the ground wake Karin from her nap. She opens her eyes and sees a blur of green, reminding her where she is. Her lifeline is wrapped around her wrist, but she grabs it too, and, grasping the platform, she turns. Peeking over the edge, she sees a group of men, chain saws in hand, staring up at her. With them there, even at this height, the tree feels safer than the ground.

"Hey, baby, what you doin?" one of the lumberjacks yells.

"Protecting this tree, to keep you from cutting it down," she answers, more defiantly than she feels.

"Be just as easy with you in it."

"More fun too," another laughs.

"Get down now if you got any sense. We're cutting our way over here, and it won't take long."

In her anger, Karin leans over. "No, it doesn't take you long. You destroy in a few hours these trees that took hundreds of years to grow."

"Look out, lady. You'll destroy yourself in minutes if you lean off your shelf. One nest egg. Scrambled."

The men leave, but the platform shakes with Karin's trembling. She takes out the CB. "This is Karin—in the tree."

"Hi," a static-filled voice from base camp responds. "You okay?"

"I guess so. Is Heather there? Or Mark?"

"No. You need anything?"

A thousand things, she thinks—more space, hot coffee, an easy way down—but all she answers is, "A friend."

"You got one here, but you better sign off. Save your batteries for emergencies."

The voice is silent; she is alone again. She puts the CB away. Munches a handful of granola. Puts the granola away. Stares into the forest, searching the trees by the river. She longs for a glimpse of Kim or Leslie, but can't see either of them.

The woods, though, come to life. Green vibrates, brilliant on the young tips of the branches reaching out of last year's darker growth. Beside the water, alders shimmer where sun caresses their new leaves. A shower of twigs falls on her head, and she looks up at a jay hopping around on a higher branch. His raspy voice has courage in it, and Karin begins to sing. Peace songs, circle songs, folk songs. Love songs from years before. Mozart arias in a range she can't reach. Holly Near in a style she can't match.

The sky turns lavender and pink, then deepens into night. Karin closes her eyes, but remains wide awake. Unfamiliar noises rise from the ground—footsteps, the snapping of twigs. Raccoons? Deer? Or coyotes and bobcats? Maybe even mountain lions; they climb trees. Maybe men. They cut them down. Owls call. She answers them with a low wail, a song of her own. And she gets through the night.

From her morning perch, Karin looks down at the sound of someone tramping through the woods—a man dressed in worn jeans and a brown jacket. He stops and glares up. Karin clutches her rope and shouts, "When are you going to stop cutting these trees?"

"When we're done. When are you gonna get out of 'em?"

"When we know they're safe." Studying him, his slight stoop, his thick, gray hair, she adds, "You must think about them too. Have you been a logger for long?"

"All my life."

"They're making you cut awfully fast now. What will you do when the trees are gone?"

"There's still plenty around," he mumbles, then turns and leaves.

The chain saws start, louder today, closer. Then the terrible scream of a falling tree, dragging the smaller ones with it as it crashes to the ground, shaking the earth, shaking her tree. Not a sound you could ever get used to, she thinks, the anguish a wave through her body. She tries to sing loudly to drown it out, but the song won't come.

At noon, the loggers saunter over. "You still around?" one of them asks. "How does it look from there?"

"It looks horrible where you're cutting," she responds. "Empty. Sad."

"So don't look. Get down and go home."

"It'll grow back," adds the man in the brown jacket.

"When? Not in our lifetime."

"Sure. America's renewable resource."

"Just like the company says," Karin's voice is shrill. "When are you going to stop listening to those North Lumber bosses and start listening to—"

"To you agitators?"

"Listen to your*selves*. The company doesn't care. They don't live here. They're in another state, another *world*. Some redwood paneled office—that's as close as they get to the trees you fall. They don't care about the trees and they don't care about you."

"They're paying us, giving us jobs."

"How long will the jobs last, logging at this rate?" Karin asks.

"North Lumber owns this property. They can do what they want with it." He shrugs. "That's the system."

In the quiet of late afternoon when the men have left the woods, other voices speak to Karin with hums and chirps and crunches. Ravens call to each other and, perhaps, to her. A beetle arrives from somewhere, landing on her arm. It is blue and green and purple, iridescent, and tickles as it walks.

Karin takes a drink, feels the water slide down her throat. Tastes it. Realizes for the first time that water has a taste. The taste of the earth, of shade, the taste of a clear spring day. Replacing the bottle, she notices her journal and picks it up to write, "Heather called on the CB. I don't know when—I don't even know how long I've been up here. Something has happened to time. Either it stopped or I'm someplace beyond it. There is day and there is night and everything is now…" The pen drops from her hand into the fold of the notebook beside a fragment of bark the tree has shed.

"Hey, you. Can you smell the coffee up there?" The loggers congregate to eat lunch and toss comments in her direction.

"My name's Karin."

"Hey Karin, come down and I'll give you coffee. I heard your friends over by the river are coming down. They're going home for the weekend. You going?"

Are they taunting her again, Karin wonders, or has something happened that base camp hasn't told her?

"You takin' the weekend off?" Now it's the gray-haired man with the brown jacket, the one they call Fred.

"No," she says. "I'm staying."

Through the windows between the branches, Karin watches the changing sky—shades of blue, shades of gray. In the wake of the sun, the ghostly light of the quarter moon silhouettes the hills, barren now where trees had been. Turning away, she burrows into her sleeping bag.

The rumble of a generator jolts her awake. Blinding searchlights invade the night, flashing through the trees. She pulls her cap down over her eyes, turns toward the shadow. The painful glare blazes around her—probing, attacking, violating. At the base of the tree, a North Lumber guard shouts above the generator's racket, "You getting down now? We brought you some light to get down."

Karin closes her eyes and hangs onto the rope. He's yelling again, but she doesn't hear his words. "Go away," she says. "Please."

She watches the searchlights withdraw, shifting toward the river, hunting the others. That will mean another day, another night, before support can bring her more supplies. She hasn't been eating much, but what she does eat is dry food, and her water is almost gone.

Fog veils the passage between night and day—damp, cold, wetting her face, seeping into her skin. She spreads her poncho over the sleeping bag and shrinks into a tighter ball, longing for the sun.

When the fog thins, she witnesses the desolation. They're cutting close, although her tree is still surrounded by others standing too near it to cut. There's another patch by the river where Kim and Leslie are sitting. As each redwood falls, Karin feels the forest's suffering. Still, she is with her tree.

Now the voices on the ground are urgent, loud.

"Karin, you gotta come down and get out of here. We're getting close, and the boss said to keep cutting."

She looks down at the men. "Who said we're more important than the trees? They don't take anything—they only give."

"Come on, we don't want you to get hurt."

"I'm part of this tree now, can't you see? If you take her, you'll have to take us both."

Fred lingers after the others have left. "I wish you'd come down."

Karin shakes her head.

"Need anything?" he asks.

"Yes. I'm out of water."

"Throw your rope down. I'll send up my canteen."

She hesitates just for a moment, then lets down her lifeline.

She hangs in the sky like a cloud, each day more a part of the world around her. She touches the thick, spongy bark and puts her ear against the tree. Can she hear the sap moving through its capillaries like the blood that moves through hers?

Her perch doesn't seem too high now that her life is connected not only with the ground but also with everything above it. The osprey feeding her young. The hummingbird who visits her red sweater. The spider whose web spans the ropes holding up her platform. The morning mist that drifts around her, and the ray of sunlight that dissolves it, as she welcomes a new day.

Contrabandista

Jane Zacharias

"Okay, let's see what you're wearing today." Female guards were the worst. This one asked Dana to turn slowly while she eyed her black boots, her scarlet jacket with the peplum.

"They're just jealous they don't look as good as we do," whispered another woman in the long visitors' line.

They inched forward and Dana checked the required transparent purse with its vending machine quarters, driver's license, and comb. Dropping her earrings into the tray, she passed through the metal detectors. *Cleared.* The big door beeped open. She crossed the sunbaked courtyard. Up the stairs into another lobby. Showed the stamped visiting pass to a guard. *Cleared.* Into the dark booth to show her wrist with its glow-in-the-dark ink to the next guard. *Cleared.*

"You're doing God's work," someone back home had said. Dana didn't know if that was true. She wasn't a minister or a social worker. But if loving was God's work, she was doing it, all right, building another wispy nest on another precarious ledge.

It had become her worn path now, the winding road from

her pretty house in Sonoma County to the state prison. Driving through the Sonoma Valley, past disciplined rows of pinot noir and chardonnay grapevines, she felt the same breathless anticipation she had felt on that other ride—the one under eucalyptus breaks and past sheep ranches to the beach place Dean had called home.

They had met in spring a year ago in a cafe near her office. He had often lounged at the counter, drinking tea and reading *The Wall Street Journal,* making eye contact as she sauntered in for a hot apple cider. She was newly free from the hostility of her second marriage, and the cafe was a safe place for some harmless trolling. He was very tall, a slender man with a weathered face and brown eyes. He had a handsome Castilian nose and an impressive blond mustache. She always returned his glance, saying "hi" as cafe regulars did.

They moved from glances to small talk. One March day soon after the equinox, Dana drove to work and parked. Crossing the lot, she felt someone gaining on her. He caught up just as she reached her office door.

"Cool day. Feels like rain," he began, still striding along. "I should introduce myself." He put out a large hand and grasped hers firmly. "Dean Mahoney." Resonant bass voice.

"Dana Peach." The moment had a genteel formality. They entered the building together.

"I sell boats. In this weather, I have lots of time to read the newspaper."

A few days later, she saw Dean Mahoney walking through her office door, heading straight for her. She watched him. "Would you like to have dinner sometime?" he asked.

"Yes." Dana was ready for this invitation.

"Tomorrow night?"

"That would be perfect." Her ex would have the kids. She was free.

"We could go out to the beach." He said he lived at the coast and mentioned a wharf restaurant.

A coworker voiced sly approval. "He looks nice. Like he might rule you, but with a velvet glove." Her name was Remy, like the cognac.

Dean met her for their date looking fresh and scrubbed, his hair wet and tousled. He wore a gray linen sport jacket and a

'50s Hawaiian shirt with pink blossoms. Dana sat on a barstool next to him looking at his hands. Huge hands, twice the size of hers, rough and creased, freckled by the sun. There were traces of grease, like he worked on cars. Competent, experienced hands. She felt attracted and at the same time, repelled.

As he talked to a friend on the barstool to his left, his right hand slid across Dana's lower back and stayed there, slowly warming her as she looked out the window at the bobbing spires of the fishing boats on the black ocean. She caught a glimpse of her face in the mirror behind the bar and was shocked by the unfamiliarity of her own smile.

He fed her like an attentive male bird and Dana let him— a bit of french bread, a scrap of artichoke, a dollop of smoked fish, each tasty tidbit delicately placed in her mouth with two of his fingers. After wine and shots of tequila, they headed onto the docks.

Out in the fresh air, they embraced and kissed, wet and smooth kisses that surpassed Dana's definition of what a good kiss should feel like. Shivering, she clutched his shoulders and leapt up, circling his waist with her legs, arching backwards, her head hanging almost over the edge of the dock. He chuckled as he pulled her up. They kissed some more.

"Want to go dancing?" he asked her between kisses.

"No."

"Well then, let's go to my place."

"Should we take two cars?" she asked.

"That depends on how much fun we want to have."

Dana locked her Jeep and clambered into his Morris station wagon. Tools and lumber crammed the back of it. Dean lit a stick of incense for the ride and in between gear shifts, held her hand. "You'll get to see first light at the beach," he said. A bright shard of moon lit their progress along the narrow coast road.

They arrived at a small house on a bluff above the beach. Tendrils of fog floated by as he unlocked the door. They passed through a chilly galley kitchen that smelled of brine and woodsmoke. Quickly, Dean switched on a radio and a small lamp, and knelt in front of the woodstove. Changing his mind, he steered Dana to the bed in a corner by five uncurtained windows overlooking the beach. In the dim light, he helped her out of her clothes, carefully undoing each covered button on her lavender shirt, slowly pulling off black lace stockings she had borrowed from Remy. Neither spoke a word.

She lay back and floated naked on his bed, her long hair fanned out on the pillow. He sat looking at her, still dressed, pink flowers blooming gaudily on his chest.

"Come on in, the water's fine. Take off your shirt—take *something* off." She helped him then, warming his bare skin with her lips, blowing lightly on his belly as she unbuttoned his jeans.

He sank down like a body surfer sensing just the right wave, and they rolled, changing places, vigorous, pushing, stretching, climbing each other as though the surface was slippery and someone might fall and perish. Suddenly, Dean sat up in the lamplight and peered anxiously at Dana.

"What is this? Where does this come from? This is not common." He shook his head. "This is uncommon!"

"Is this weird for you, a strange woman in your house with you tonight?"

"No! My little house is starved for the likes of you."

Dana could hardly believe her good fortune. They'd rest and be ready to catch another wave. Outside the ocean seethed and boiled as the tide crept closer. At last they lay under a pile of soft old quilts, sharing sleepy snippets about their lives. "Only been separated a year. It's tough. Scrambling to keep the house. Happier. I can breathe," Dana murmured. "Marriage not my strong suit. A good mother, yes. Down deep, I'm a loner."

Dean tallied his possessions like a tribesman—the wine cellar, vintage car, ivory for carving—a rich litany. "Fellow like me, content as a beach bum. Surfing since I was a little kid." Dana lay with her back snuggled tightly against the fur on his chest, savoring the liquid play of his fingers between her legs when he whispered the word *contrabandista*.

"Matter of fact, I'll probably be doing time soon, hopefully county time. I was stopped with an ounce or so of toot in my car. Arrested for transportation."

He lived on the edge of a cold ocean populated with hardcore surfers and the occasional great white shark. She lived on the edge of a field populated with deer and live oaks. Dean had California roots; Dana was an immigrant from a frigid northern province. Both were wiry as whippets, both were curious and thrifty, both loved anchovies.

Dana had been around the block a few times since her valedictory address at the college for daughters of the elite.

She'd developed a penchant for the unconventional. That summer, she welcomed Dean's wary courtship and accepted, even relished, the long spaces between each rendezvous.

She grew wild with yearning, remembering him intent in candlelight, trimming the wick to her oil lamp. The sight of his tall frame at her office door, the rumble of his voice, "I sold a car, I bought a boat," told her all was right with the world. Just when she decided he wouldn't call again, he'd surface in the cafe. "Wait, I almost forgot," he'd say, pulling a gardenia blossom the color of clotted cream from between the pages of the business section. When his fingers grazed her inner thigh, she felt her nipples harden into bullets.

She knew there were other loyalties, women he'd known long before he'd met her. She worried about the brunette with the ugly handbag she'd seen having breakfast with him in the cafe. But with Dean, Dana buried her usual feistiness and swallowed her insecurities whole. His whole demeanor told her not to ask.

"Oh, oh," said Remy one day. "Sex and drugs."

"It's not that simple," Dana snapped. She and Dean were tripping, but it wasn't drugs. She'd get a call from a phone booth, traffic roaring in the background like the ocean itself.

"Can you meet me at the beach?" he'd ask. An hour later, she'd be standing in his kitchen, mincing garlic. He'd be patting tortillas on the griddle with one hand, sneaking the other hand under her skirt like a spy retrieving secret instructions.

Then they'd slide down like two snakes coiling on hot asphalt. Taking clothes off didn't matter. Neither did kissing. She kept her eyes wide open watching him make love to her. Sometimes his eyes met hers. Mostly, he was rapt, like Eric Clapton playing his guitar.

Summer waned. The best lawyer around advised Dean to forget county time. Dean pled guilty. A parade of witnesses vouched for his solid character. Unconvinced, the judge frowned. "You're a businessman, not an addict," he said. "Dean Francis Mahoney, I sentence you to five years in the state penitentiary."

Dean was stoic. "It'll be less. Don't worry, sweetie. I'll be out in no time."

It was September. The pastures on the way to the beach had turned yellow. Coyote brush was sweetly pungent, naked ladies nodded by the side of the road. Dana felt the ache of leave-taking as she drove to Dean's the last time, savoring the sight of his house on the bluff with its own swirling weather, the sun leaving a pink smear as it dropped into the sea. Van Morrison sang "Into the Mystic" on the radio as she silently wrapped his grandmother's china teacups in newspaper. In the morning, they lingered in bed.

"Make it all go away," he whispered while she memorized every angle and line of his body with her mouth.

At home, she suffered a gusty crying fit. Her children paced like panthers outside her closed bedroom door.

Trembling, she wrote him a letter.

> *I like you Dean, but when I first see you, I shake. Why is this? I'd rather be the casual one, but I warned you, I'm intense. Perhaps in my next lifetime, I'll be cool. I'm a sensualist. I like the taste of your food and your grace in sharing it—chocolate-covered strawberries placed warm in my mouth, Carpinteria oranges, the perfect avocado ripening on your sill. I like that you make jam. I'm moved by your grandfatherly gentleness and the guarded look in your eyes. I will miss seeing you having tea and reading the newspaper in the cafe, but I'm happy that you have touched me. Do you think about these things?*

> *This is not a love letter.*

Dana stopped. With careful precision, she whited out *not*.

Dean's letters showed up in Dana's mailbox with uncharacteristic speed. Calligraphy and rosebuds decorated the envelopes. His heart was smiling at the memory of her, he said. But while he was detained in a high security facility, he forbade her visits. "Talking on phones through glass is not pleasant. Don't come."

Four months into his sentence he sent the news. *Application cleared for contact visits.* Now, every other Saturday, she rose in the chilly predawn and groomed herself for her lover. Nothing denim, you'd get turned away. High heels with textured stockings were good. The desired effect was feminine, not tawdry, or the guards' shit detectors would go off. No skirts above the knee. No tank tops. A dab of sandalwood oil. Crystal earrings to catch the light. Silk to soothe the sensibility of an incarcerated artist, the man who had once told Dana she looked as sleek as a Ferrari. Some days, an orchid for the man who had cultivated flowers.

He was slow to warm to her the first time in the smoky cacophany of the visiting room. Could this be the author of the tender letters? Dana persevered.

> *In your letter you said I'm asking for and getting nothing. How visiting feels like a chaperoned dance at your boys' parochial school. This juiciness I feel is for you, and with your invitation, I bring it to you. No, you're not wearing your Hawaiian shirt or hand-feeding me sushi. Instead, people around us are eating little tubs of microwaved beef stew, all the men are in blue, babies are bleating in their makeshift pens while their desperate parents cop a feel. I'm breathing some killer's secondhand smoke but Dean, I'm on fire for you!*

Dana watched Dean through opaque windows, his hands up in surrender while a guard frisked him. Tall Dean, ducking under the door, headed for her.

Kissing had become an art for them. The work of lips and tongues was something the guards never monitored. Sitting in an inmate's lap—forbidden. Touching genitals—possible, but risky. Each caress had an aching caution. But kissing—*that* a man could pursue and still maintain dignity.

Now it was Dean with his eyes open as he kissed Dana, scanning the guards as they patrolled the outdoor courtyard. Slowly, he pulled away and leaned back in his chair. Together they watched the promenade, inmates circling with their ladies, seagulls swooping down to score a Cheeto. Dana brought his fingertips into her mouth, meeting them with her tongue. Just as carefully, she guided the hand into her skirt pocket, through the wide cut she had made this morning.

"Mornin' Mahoney. Mornin' Miss." The guard continued his stroll.

Dean's fingers found her skin and stretched across her thigh. Dana watched with pleasure as his pale face subtly changed color and his gaze met hers.

The Flavor of Disaster

Noelle Oxenhandler

When I was a child growing up in California, we didn't worry about earthquakes. We worried about the Russians. Only a few years ago I returned to California, to Sonoma County, after many years in upstate New York. And what I marvel at is how seamlessly The Big One has taken over for The Bomb. At school, my daughter and her little friends have learned to crouch beneath their desks at the first rumble of earthquake, just as we did in the '50s, practicing for The Bomb.

Unlike other forms of disaster—blizzards, hurricanes, tornadoes—the quintessential feature of both The Bomb and The Big One is that they can happen at any time. They can happen on a beautiful day. And because the days are so often beautiful here in California, this imparts a very particular flavor to the expectation of disaster.

As a child, running down the beach in Santa Monica under a luminous sky, I would say to myself, "All this is about to explode," and it was as though the imminent horror itself was contained within the sunlight, the blue water, the smell of lotion. This simultaneously thrilling and unbearable tension of opposites is exactly the same as that produced by the constant expectation of earthquake—and it is nearly impossible to live with moment by moment. Is it any wonder that we Californians are famous for our forgetfulness? We are famous, too, for the more defiant stance of hedonism: the voluptuousness of slowly turning golden brown as the earth waits, buckling, below the beach towel. But underneath these clichés there is something that I believe to be much deeper, and much more quintessentially Californian. It is the unshakable belief that what makes every pleasure both possible and more acute is the fact that, contained within it, is the possibility of total annihilation.

When I was eight, I was chosen from my class to be on *The Art Linkletter Show.* A limousine came to pick up the three of us who, so our teacher said, had not been "bumps on a log" on the day the talent scouts made their sweep. The chauffeur in his navy blue cap drove us to the studio in Hollywood, and it was one of the few times that I had actually been into the heart of the city. I had rarely been among so many tall buildings, so inevitably, as we stepped into the dark back rooms of the studio, I imagined them all exploding into rubble around me. But it wasn't just because the buildings were so tall that I had an even more heightened sense of apocalypse than usual. Rather, it was precisely because I was being treated so royally. Once the limousine brought us to the studio, a nice lady took me into a little booth and asked me questions. Then, basking under stage lights before a sea of applauding adults, all I had to do was repeat for Art the very same lines that the lady had promised me would be funny. What did I want to be when I grew up? "A pianist." (The very word, from a child's mouth, drew laughter.) What was the most important thing a pianist should remember? "Always wash your hands before playing or they'll stick to the piano." Afterwards, we were taken to lunch at an elegant restaurant with air-conditioning and a pastry cart. I spent a long time choosing my pastry and finally decided on an eclair. In the taste of the whipped cream I found again, in its most concentrated form, what I had found so many times in the sunlight when I ran down the beach beside the sparkling water: the perpetual imminence of The Bomb.

And only a few days ago, pressing my face deep into the petals and leaves of a wet lilac tree in my backyard in Glen Ellen, I had a similar experience. Having lived for so long in the Snowbelt, I still have to get used to the profusion of blossoms that comes after so little winter suffering. When I am out among the flowers, I tend to feel anxious and oddly disoriented, as though all were not right with the world. But as I breathed in the smell of the purple blossoms, I finally felt something settle. At a cellular level I retrieved what is for me more ancient than the movement from snow to flowers: the primal presence of disaster. The name of the expected disaster has changed, but it ' is that presence which, from my earliest memories, both permits and intensifies my experience of earthly delight. Strange and paradoxical as it might seem, it is the perpetual imminence of earthquake which—in this otherwise so beautiful and benevolent spot—now maintains my sense of balance in the cosmos.

I know, of course, from the three moderate earthquakes I have actually experienced, how easily this "sense of balance" can give way to terror. For even these were enough to make me understand that one of the most emotionally unsettling things about earthquakes is the way they negate the natural human impulse to take shelter. Where can an earthling go when the earth itself is shaking? We are taught to crouch under tables or doorways, but the strategy provides very little imagined comfort. Now finally we encounter a crucial difference between The Big One and The Bomb. For in the era of The Bomb we could still cling (quite absurdly) to the primal identification of ground and home with safety, and most of the people I knew had their very own bomb shelters on the ground floor.

It is here, in the memory of those shelters, that something like nostalgia arises for the pervasive fear of my childhood. There was a great variety of shelters. Some of them were quite serious, set up in clean, cement-block garages or cold, dark basements and outfitted with rows of shelves holding sensible items for survival. Others were fanciful. Our neighbors, the McDonnels, had a hidden shelter inside their house, along the stairwell. To find the secret door, you had to move a large oil painting of a Spanish Madonna. She was a beautiful lady with big, long-lashed eyes and a black lace mantilla that hung from the dark, upswept hair above her forehead all the way down to her shoulders. She seemed both glamorous and serene, and actually I wasn't sure if she was a Madonna or a flamenco dancer. Behind the door there was a dark windowless space with a dirt floor, and as there were no supplies in there I never knew how the McDonnels, who had six children, were planning to survive. They were a very devout family, however—it was Mary Kay McDonnel who, when we were six, had taught me to make the sign of the cross over myself every time I heard a siren—and somehow there was the feeling in their bomb shelter that they didn't need supplies. They would simply crouch and pray under the protection of the Flamenco Madonna.

My own family's bomb shelter was quite a different matter. My parents were cynical about the Cold War mentality, and it was only quite begrudgingly, and long after all the neighbors had theirs, that my mother gave in and fashioned us a sort of shelter in her closet. I had always been fascinated by her closet, which was actually a tiny boudoir with a cushioned stool and a built-in dressing table with a mirror. I loved to see her clothes, hanging like a procession of her different selves, and all smelling to me like her mocha lipstick. I loved to look through the collection of small boxes that, set on a tray on the dressing table, held her jewels—including the coiled gold snake bracelet that Great-Uncle John had brought back to Great-Aunt Maria from the Orient, and the black onyx crucifix which, mysteriously, had carved upon it a green nymph with a water vase. Every now and again, looking around for something she'd said I could borrow, a scarf or maybe a tortoiseshell comb for my hair, I would peer into other, forbidden drawers and glimpse some secret article of feminine hygiene whose name and function were unknown to me. Though I never stayed very long, because of the feeling of trespass that would overcome me, that closet was an initiatory space for me. If I were ever to stay there long enough, surely I would come to know what it was to be a woman, and what was the mysterious power that drew men and women close.

And now, into this small place of glamour and important secrets, came an odd collection of survival items: a portable toilet, toilet paper, and bottled water from France. As a kind of protest, my mother refused to add anything else of practical value to our stash. Instead, whenever my Grandmother Billie sent any of the strange gourmet foods that were her regular holiday gift, my mother put them directly into the bomb shelter. She had long complained that these expensive, and to us quite inedible treats—the tinned reindeer meat from Norway, the pickled roe, and marinated hearts of bamboo—simply cluttered up the kitchen, but that she couldn't bring herself to get rid of them. At last she had found the perfect solution: she could whisk them out of sight immediately, while simultaneously contributing to our survival in time of holocaust.

All this came back to me when, in the wake of the last Los Angeles earthquake, our sense of perpetually possible disaster was once again heightened. Sonoma County rests on several large and active faults, and in the general spirit of urgency, my daughter's school sent home an informational packet. The cover letter urged parents to organize for earthquake emergency and asked us to prepare a little comfort-kit for our children. In the kit we were supposed to put a small stuffed animal and a loving message.

My daughter, who was seven at the time, had no trouble picking out a small, cheery-looking penguin to go in the ziplock bag, but I spent a long time composing the message. It is hard to find the words to tell one's child in the aftermath of a disaster that has not yet happened. Finally I decided on:

> Dear Ariel,
> WOW! What a big boom that was. That was scary, wasn't it? Are you still shaking? We know that they are going to take good care of you at your school, and we will come to get you just as soon as we can. Meanwhile, is there another child who is smaller than you who is feeling really scared? Maybe you can make them feel a little better, because you're good at doing that. Later, you can tell us all about it. And meanwhile, remember to take big, deep BREATHS....
> We love you and we'll get there as soon as we can....

Though they hadn't told us to include a treat, I couldn't help adding a bar of dark Swiss chocolate to the bag, and when I showed Ariel she seemed pleased. Having completed the comfort-kit and sent it off to school, I turned to the next task: putting together a stash of supplies that could be safely stored outside our house. I cleaned out a large, plastic garbage bin and let it air a day or two in the sunlight. Inside it I put two wool blankets, three heavy-duty flashlights, six gallon-jugs of bottled water, toilet paper, and matches.

Then I went to the grocery store to buy food. I walked up and down the aisles for a long time. I put things in my cart, then took them out again. At last I settled on Ak-Mak crackers, which seemed somehow appropriately Biblical, and several packages of mixed dried fruit. I bought a jar of olives to complete the Biblical motif, and a tin of Scottish shortbread for a special treat. My decisions seemed momentous to me—and is it any wonder? Already I knew that for my daughter, Earthquake would inevitably conjure the image of a small penguin and the odor of dark chocolate—just as for me, Nuclear Holocaust meant—among so many terrible things that I could not dare to imagine—the smell of salt water and sun lotion, whipped cream, my Grandmother Billie's tinned reindeer meat, precious jewels, and the mystery of sex between my mother and father.

Fog Dance

Liza Prunuske

Cool air flows in
like water. We drink it.
Lady dog sleeps with deep
slow breaths. Harvest moon,
full moon, partial eclipse. Baby,
you are welcome.

Fog fills Coleman Valley.
Rain smell, naked
full-bellied woman
dancing for rain, dancing for her thirsty
redwoods, for the shrunken bay trees
in Cazadero, for the aching throats
of small streams.

My belly rises and hardens
as if it might pull itself
off my body, fly away.
If you looked into this house,
you would see small pools
of light. The fog climbs
above the tree line, sinks,
then rises again.
We breathe together,
the fog, my belly, and I.

Calavero Beach

Air that is nothing,
air that is everything
lift the raven's wings,
be blanket of nothing
between its small tough bones
and the curling water.

Carry the pulse
of breakers, the cormorants'
soft crackle. Disperse
the downy seed
of *Cirsium occidentale*,
wild, red thistle.

Seven years ago
I came here to breathe.
My daughter turned
inside me
and then lay still, asleep
on her bed of water.
Three days later
she was born into air
to confound her brother
and rise
sudden as an alder seedling.

She can see over oceans,
owns every red flower.
Her breath
can steady wings.

October

The time of deer running,
brown on brown hills,
of wanting to be somewhere else.

Of wanting to be
what in secret
we are.

In the morning
we remember leaping
over fences. Our beds smell
like dry grass,
like wind.

Liza Prunuske

My Phantom Heart

Robin Beeman

The spirit lingers on for three days, they say, and so I have.
I'm lingering, not quite sure what I am and occasionally feeling
uneasy about this nether state. I still have not a clue as to what
will come next. I seem to be a mist of some sort—slightly
soggy and clingy—though I do not remember myself as that
sort of person in life. Now, however, I want to cling to everything. Day three is almost over.

They've chosen sunset for this little event, about forty people standing around a mound of flowers, in a cove just north of
Salmon Creek. Almost everyone is here, from my daughter, my
girlfriends, some friends from work, several former lovers
including my daughter's father, my landlord, and my boss at
the restaurant where I kept the books. What an odd job to
wind up in. It seems I was good with numbers.

Almost everyone is here but my son Beau, my darling
Kama Sutra's brother. Little Rainbow, what a sweet kid he was.
He took to calling himself Beau in high school. His father was
electrocuted in a hot tub when the stereo he was listening to
fell into the water during an earthquake. It was only a 4.2, so
don't believe those stories that little quakes are harmless.

My ashes, grainy silver stuff containing nuggets of bone
resembling sea-worn shell, rest in a gold foil box with a wild iris
taped to the top. My favorite flower. How lucky I was to die in
the spring when they bloom. The iris on the box was Kama
Sutra's idea, and I give her credit for being too distressed to
realize just how tacky the box is. She is truly torn up and that
breaks what I'll have to call my "phantom heart" for lack of a
better word. In a happier mood she might have thought to
decant the ashes into something classier—one of Rae's vases

maybe, with a bit of plastic wrap over the top. She's very possessive of my ashes, keeping them beside her as she slept last night. I was touched. I was in my Indian phase when she was born, hence the name. She's been quite a good girl. Nothing like the kind of girl I was. But my days were different days, were they not?

Not that I planned to die at all—though I knew I probably would someday. If I could have, I would certainly have planned my demise via some more elegant manner than tripping over the cat and bonking my head on the corner of the cast iron stove. That damn cat. She never liked me. She's spent the last two nights curled up beside Kami, the name my daughter choose in eighth grade when she decided the implications of Kama Sutra were something of a burden. Kami thought the animal was grieving, but I know better.

I don't remember anything after hitting the stove except that suddenly I found myself trying to emerge from a body lying on the floor, an act which felt very much like trying to get out of a tight wetsuit.

There, dampness again. Well, we are at the coast. My little cottage is right over the ridge behind that stand of redwoods. Such a sweet little place. Such low rent. I'd lived there for years and planned on many more.

Rick is here in an Italian suit out of some sense of decorum only he would imagine. His feet are bare, his Gucci loafers in the trunk of the Jag. He's living in Los Angeles now. Up here in Sonoma county, I don't think I know anyone with any kind of suit. Oh, Rick. We came out here together from Iowa in '67. From the cornfields to the Haight. He'd been my boyfriend but then suddenly he was a musician—though not a very good one. Then later, when things started to shift in the early '80s, he was suddenly an agent. Of course, my singing days were over by then. Not that I had much of a career.

"She could have been a star," he's whispering to Melissa. I did sing backup for some of the very best groups, the Orange Bananas first, then the Ripe Skeletons. I even sang backup for Dylan once.

"She was a star," Melissa says.

Kami's eyes are moist. It is pollen season, but we're at the coast and the breeze is from the west so maybe they're real tears. Jason is next to her—her father—still a hunk. Carpenters stay that way. I loved his hands. That muscle between his thumb and forefinger—I can't remember the name though there is one—all those muscles have names—just drove me wild. Just let me kiss you there I'd say. Nice guy. A bit of a flake, but flakiness in the grand scheme of things—though I'm still not privy to the big picture if there is one—is a relatively minor sin. We didn't get married, out of principle. Then he went on to marry three times, all women with money. I don't think he's greedy though, just not highly motivated. He likes to work, but only on his schedule. He's checking the sky, the wind, trying to decide if there'll be surf tomorrow. I wonder what his current wife thinks of him. Now he's asking Kami if she has any Advil. It seems he has a touch of bursitis in his right shoulder.

I search the crowd again for some sign of Beau, but no. Kami finally found someone to leave a message with in Ketchikan. I hope he's all right, which means I am still worrying about him. This mother stuff is probably the last to go.

Kami no doubt thinks—funny I can see everything but I can't read minds—that as soon as my ashes are out there I'll lose no time mingling with the elements—slightly sentient, at least for a while—until I'm taken in by phytoplankton. She's very into natural cycles, my little Gaia.

Rick is probably wondering if I'm getting to meet the big ones—Jimi, Janis, Jerry—in that fine old backstage in the sky. Maybe I should have changed my name to something with a J. Margaret Ann was just so Midwestern that I decided to call myself Ocean as soon as I waded into that icy foam right at the end of Golden Gate Park. But lately I'd found myself asking people to call me Margaret Ann again. I wonder if that was significant, a sign that the big surprise was on its way.

My girlfriends are standing together. Song, Melissa, Judith, and Rae. A good bunch. Melissa and Judith are no doubt wondering who'll I'll come back as. Judith was sure we'd once all been warrior women riding horses and shooting arrows. After her mastectomy, she refused to have a reconstruction because she said a breast would interfere with her shooting arm. Song, on the other hand, said if she lost a breast she'd like them both redone, size C.

Melissa was the one who found me. She'd come over to return my copy of *Emma*. We were into English novels these days—a big relief. I think if I'd had to read another self-help book or anything else by a guru, I'd have become a turnip. So much of that became so simple-minded after a while. They all made everything sound so easy, which wasn't always the case. I'd come to believe I'd learn more from fiction.

I had a copy of *Middlemarch* on the table, but truly I'd been having trouble getting into it though I knew I would appreciate it by the end. I was going to ask Melissa to give me a pep talk about it. Melissa teaches English in high school. Jane Austen was no problem though. A lady with her wits about her. Maybe I would get to meet Jane in the beyond, if there is such a place. Maybe she and Janis were girlfriends already, singing together. Maybe they'd let me sit in. Jane might have a hell of a voice—something that didn't work well with a pianoforte but would be outstanding with a guitar.

Melissa called her homeopath, who came over and pronounced me dead. Good Lord, rigor was already setting in, Melissa. But Melissa likes someone in authority to pronounce on things. Next, she called Kami up from Berkeley where she's getting a Ph.D. in biology. Kami arrived in time for the washing, which honestly she wasn't that pleased about. You know how daughters are about mothers' bodies. They had me laid out on the table and Melissa whipped up a concoction of herbs—rosemary for remembrance and rue for something else. I might have been poor drowned Ophelia instead of somebody with an egg-sized lump from a fall. Thank goodness the lump was on my temple, so that with a little artful hair styling everything looked fine. Kami washed my hands and feet and my face. Judith, a nurse, and Rae, just plain unflappable, did the privates. Melissa got very hung up washing my abdomen—my mother earth belly, I guess. Song picked out the clothes. I'd given up the gypsy look years ago but she had me in an Indian cotton blouse and a multicolored skirt with beads—lots of beads. Kami made sure I was wearing my Birkenstocks. Then she got on the phone trying to reach Beau, up in Alaska on a fishing boat. She stayed on the phone for hours, calling one number after another with no luck.

I was very moved by all their caring, though by then I was out of the wetsuit and already becoming detached emotionally from the old carcass. It had served me well, however. A sturdy body—never really slim, but good for giving birth in a tipi overlooking the Russian River. A very good body for eating and drinking and lovemaking. And very good for hiking and swimming. How freckled my arms and hands had gotten. Too much sun. But the rest of me was doing well, only a few strands of gray in that long red hair. One small consolation for going so soon, barely fifty, was that I wouldn't have to save up for anything cosmetic like Rae and Song were doing.

I'm saying now that I was feeling detached but there were moments. I really thought I'd have a stroke, if I could have then, watching that cardboard box holding what was left of me slide into the oven at the crematorium, just another big log on the fire. I was cringing even though there was nothing to cringe with. I went outside and waited for my smoke, which was a nice pale plume—nontoxic, I hope, and not too polluting.

Rick has his guitar and he begins singing "Brown Eyed Girl," doing his best Van Morrison imitation, which is none too good. Has he forgotten I had green eyes?

Jason brought a friend who also has a guitar. He plays next and he's very good, as he sings, "Wonderful Tonight." I've always been a sucker for Eric Clapton. If I could have cried, I would have.

Bruno, my most recent ex-boyfriend, is there in the back, looking miserable, as well he should. We'd been going together for years but when I suggested we get married—a girl should get married at least once in her life—he started making excuses.

Rae, bless her heart, takes over the next phase. She talks briefly about what a good friend I was and what a good mother —both of which I hope are true to some degree. "She liked to make oatmeal cookies with raisins and walnuts," Rae says. "We could never leave her house without a bag of oatmeal cookies to take home." What an odd thing to remember. I guess that was to show that I was a nurturing human being, but as best I can recall I made oatmeal cookies a dozen times in my entire life, if that many.

The wind is picking up and there's a suggestion of fog moving down from the mouth of the river. Rae says if anyone in the group wants to step forward to do it now and to keep it brief. I do love that about Rae—practical. She mentions that scattering ashes on a beach is illegal—which I wasn't aware of—but that we should feel good about doing something illegal in memory of all the marches and sit-ins and demonstrations we took part in during what she calls "the good old days."

I suddenly realize I don't have to stick around. That I can move away. It's pleasant drifting along over the water's edge. I can see Bodega Head and the crab boats on their way into the harbor. I'll miss it all. The wind dies down and I waft back. They are facing the ocean now. The sun appears from under the clouds and adds its note of glory. I find myself drawn to its deep carmine color. It's tugging me ever so slightly. I seem to be getting lighter, drier.

I turn for another glimpse. Kami and Jason are both sobbing. I always knew Kami loved me, but is it possible that Jason really loved me too? Could he have been the love of my life? How odd to discover this now. Maybe we could have worked things out. "I love you," I'm trying to say, but all I'm doing is making a puff of breeze.

Rae and Melissa begin singing "Amazing Grace." Beautiful harmony. The rest join in. A good song to leave on. After the first stanza, the sound of a motorcycle breaks in. Beau. He parks, tears off his helmet, letting his long red curls fly as he runs to the beach. I guess I don't have to worry about him. He embraces Kami and stands beside her looking out over the water as if he can see me.

Kami gives the iris to Beau, then opens the box. She flings its contents, a sandy silver shower, into the air. At that exact same moment the wind gusts up again sending a dusting of me over every one of the gathered.

I think they're saying goodbye but I can't really hear. I'm certainly getting lighter. Yes, much lighter. Goodbye, I'm calling. Another puff of breeze, sailing toward the shore.

Purple Haze

Delia Moon

"Here," breathed Delia. "This is what I want. Here."

And so it came to pass that a piece of land was bought because of a running pebbled stream, winding and brown under fallen branches of alder and bay in the greenfern grove. Because her husband Sandy's eyes had met hers and they had said, "Here we will start Community." Because it was near where, on a walk some years before, she had heard a voice from her heart say she would die here. Die here. Die here.

It was in the last years of the flame of youth that Delia created her community. Now Delia is walking beside this same stream in twilight in the last of her middle years, dreaming again of community, of Purple Haze, where old folks, women, artists, will come to lean on each other in their age and infirmity, to draw strength from their nearness, to joyfully interweave their dreams

Where are the men in Delia's fantasy? They are not there. She doesn't know quite why. Perhaps they have succumbed to the inevitable statistic, perhaps they were not there to begin with, or perhaps the women are partnered with women as she now is. Perhaps the men will be there after all and she doesn't yet see them. She sees women howling at the autumn moon in concert, dancing arm-in-arm or cheek-to-cheek, breast-to-breast beneath the buckeye tree.

Now, as she approaches the end of her sixth decade, a woman who lives alone with her dog in a meadow by a creek, hoping to be followed by a partner, then others, she is pleased that her friends Salli and Annie, have joined her dream and said, "Let's make this a reality!"

At present there is a barn, elegantly positioned in the meadow by the creek. This barn may one day house Purple Haze so Delia and others who share the dream can live together near neighbors, friends and children. Others have imagined Purple Haze already. Robin wants to join, and Sarah, and Louise and the many others whose eyes shine at the prospect of growing old in community.

Time alone will tell if Purple Haze will hold aging bodies and souls in shared contentment. Meanwhile, Delia dreams.

The Coffin Garden

Salli Rasberry

I awoke at two in the morning three years ago, just before my birthday, and realized I was going to die. It was as clear as pure water. At some point my life would come to an end. There would be no more dancing with my husband at the Fourth of July picnic, no more singing country western on the freeway, no more sunsets at the beach, no more writing books, no more making love, no more snuggles with my grandbabies. I lay there somewhere between panic and despair, trapped in the tape loop of my life. At daybreak I sighed deeply into the bathroom mirror, a woman of a certain age looking over her shoulder. My head was full of butterflies.

My father died alone thirty years ago of heart failure in a veterans' hospital in Chillicothe, Ohio. I was not invited to his funeral. My mother told me there was no need to come home. I was a flower child in the Haight-Ashbury counter-culture, a single mom with a small child of my own. I had no money and no one offered to send me a ticket. I was not there to grieve with everyone else. I heard the church overflowed with people who loved my father but I missed the funeral of the man who gave me life and whose death I am just beginning to mourn. I didn't understand at the time why it was so important to grieve with others. My dad went to heaven in Cincinnati and that was that.

How could it be that I never dealt with the death of my father? How could it be that I never considered my own death? I live in a community where birthing ways, home births and hand-crafted wedding ceremonies are a part of life. Did I think good food, exercise, and a caring heart would carry me through to the final goodbye?

I got online to discover death in cyberspace. I found an assisted-suicide website, grief chat rooms, the Memorial Garden where one could send virtual flowers, and caskets made to order. I heard a lot of bad funeral stories. At Copperfield's, I found a plethora of books but not one that spoke to me, counter-culture-baby-boomer looking for the magical blend of stories, practical information, and inspirational ritual. I decided to write my own book.

I felt I needed to do more than talk and write about death—I needed to be physically involved. With the help of friends I created the Coffin Garden, dedicated to celebrating the cycle of life. I hoped that putting it into the creative realm would help me die with grace and consciousness.

The first year we planted hundreds of sunflowers. There were so many that the stalks grew thin to make room for them all. They leaned on each other for support—a mass of brilliant orange, brown, and yellow. The next year my husband built twelve coffin-shaped planter boxes and arranged them in a circle like giant flower petals. By summer, each coffin overflowed with flowers and vegetables.

Now, when you walk under the sign of weathered redwood inscribed "Bloom Where You Are Planted," the Silver Lace vine wrapped around the trellis envelops you in coolness. The view is of verdant hillsides, the town of Bodega to the west and Freestone to the north. You can almost see the ocean. We have made a small altar in honor of my father. It's a peaceful place where you can quietly contemplate life and death as you look out over the valley below. It is here in the Coffin Garden that I hope to have my memorial service.

As part of my memorial I have started painting a long canvas of my life that can be spread out like a carpet for the mourners to walk upon barefooted. On either side of the canvas, my husband and daughter will stand and welcome our friends into the garden. I will be laid beneath a lattice bower made of balsa wood and covered with flowers in hues of blues, pinks, and purples gathered from the gardens of my friends. I will wear a long gown made of pure cotton and embroidered with tiny roses, violets, and lilies of the valley.

I hope I will be able to die at home at peace with myself. I would like my friends to dress me and brush my hair, massage my feet and hands. I want to surrender gracefully. I don't want any undertaker to make a mask of my face.

My friends and extended family, who are a very talented bunch, will do little skits, sing songs, and play music together. I hope those gathered will sing "Red River Valley," "Eagle When She Flies," and "Will the Circle Be Unbroken." After the service the canvas will be rolled up like a scroll and given to my daughter and her children. I take pleasure in imagining my grandchildren unrolling the scroll with their mother on the anniversary of my death and reminiscing about Grammy. As those I love gather to help my spirit pass, I want them to find strength and joy in this ceremony and to celebrate their own lives.

I am determined to help bring death out of the closet and shamelessly inflict my new death awareness on friends and even strangers. I am grateful that I had my death dream and for all that has followed. It has helped me appreciate my relationships and community so much more. I have become more tolerant. I say I love you more often. When I awaken now from the cocoon of sleep I feel as delicately balanced as a dandelion tuft in a summer breeze.

Michele

Annie Wells

I felt like a student/child listening to a teacher/mother as I sat at her feet during her illness. She was so lucid and candid about her life and her death.

I lost my mother to breast cancer at eighteen. My family didn't address anything that was charged with any emotion. I was completely unprepared for her death and have spent years trying to come to terms with it

During my career as a photojournalist I have sought out stories about death and dying to help me understand.

Michele Moser became my mother, kindly and gently telling me about the pain of death and about a certain ultimate beauty in life. I can't put words to this feeling. I only know that I felt uplifted every time I saw her—even the day she told me she wouldn't see me again. When I left I hugged and kissed her. Even stuck my head back in the door to blow her a kiss. Even hollered goodbye back to her as she said goodbye one more time as I walked beneath her window, like a good friend who is leaving on a trip, but will be back.

Rescue

Although this photo is newspaper photography at its most intense—a witnessing of extreme human endeavor—at another reading it takes on the substance of a myth. A young woman on the cusp of womanhood is drowning in life's torrential river and is saved by a virile, handsome man. Too much? Maybe. But that truth lives in this picture and I think gives it a power in addition to the heroic fact that a person is risking his life to save another.

I would never have made that photo if Janielle Jobe, my editor at *The Press Democrat*, had not sent me out after it. Janielle heard the call on the police scanner and called me off another assignment. I owe my Pulitzer to her good news judgment. She died of ovarian cancer two months after I took the photo. She left behind a wonderful husband and two little girls. I hope that when the girls are older and looking for answers about who they are and wonder about their mother and what kind of person she was, they will realize that she was an integral part of the most esteemed award in her profession.

The Grateful Living

Pam Cobb

Until Megan met Diane at the Fisherman's Cafe, she was certain no other person alive could relate to her world. As they swapped stories that day, Megan knew they shared more than being single and working on commercial salmon boats in Bodega Bay.

"Sometimes when the weather's calm and the fish aren't biting, I decide to leave my body," Diane said casually.

"You're kidding." Megan was in awe.

"No, I just hang out up on top of the mast and watch the whole show."

"And I thought I was radical, throwing the *I Ching* every morning so I could tell Captain Frank which direction to go."

When the winds howled off the Bodega Head and it was too rough to fish, Megan and Diane followed tradition and spent mornings at the Fisherman's Cafe, swapping stories of fishing, fisherman, boats, and weather.

"Did you ever notice, Diane, that when a guy loses a fish, it's never even mentioned, but when you do, it's all that girl stuff? 'Girls aren't strong enough. Women are bad luck on boats. They smell too much like fish. Yuk, yuk!'"

They squealed in delight and then lowered their voices as the fishermen turned and stared.

"Ned actually came over to the boat last night and asked if I'd like to go into town to Marty's and have a few drinks."

"Ned? The one with three kids, Ned?" Megan asked.

"Yeah, that Ned."

"So what did you say?"

"What do you think? No, of course, that slimy cheating scumbag."

"And what did he say?"

"That he always knew."

"Always knew what?"

"That I was a lesbian." Their muffled laughter did not go unnoticed.

"You can't win either way, Diane. When I first came to Bodega Bay, I made the humongous mistake of having sex with…" Megan leaned towards Diane and whispered. "Sea Mist Tom."

"Noooo," Diane's eyes widened into little spaceships, whirling in disbelief. "What a highliner that kid is."

"Not to mention gorgeous. Tom had a knowledge of fishing I would *die* for. Well, grovel for."

"So did he give you any hot tips?"

"He did show me how to make perfect bait which has made a big difference. And one night, while Tom was sleeping and I was lying there in my usual make-sure-the-anchor-isn't-dragging half-awake state, he shouts out, 'Purple hoochies.' And sure enough, the next day those salmon bit the heck out of purple hoochies. He said I was special and those nights together our little secret. Then, one evening, I was flipping through the upper CB channels, the so-called secret ones, that's when I heard him giving some other guy the intimate details of our sex life. They get those channels all the way to Mexico, Diane. I was mortified."

"Actually, I first heard about you from a fishermen out of Ensenada."

"Very funny. What really grabs me is that every one of them is out there with a male deckhand for eight to ten days at a time and that's just fine, but the few times a boat pulls in here with two women, they're goddamn lesbians."

"Well, when we get our own boat, we'll deliver fish in leather miniskirts and high-heeled boots—then they can really wonder."

They shrieked and high-fived each other. Heads turned and shook in bewilderment.

Megan had to admit, as much as she complained about the little things—the clothes that never dried, the smell of diesel, the long hours, and frequent feelings of isolation—she never doubted that this was the life for her. She had felt like a prisoner at her secretarial job in San Francisco, trapped within the walls of a cubicle with a computer eight hours a day. She loved being outdoors, doing physical labor, breathing the clean salt air, and eating salmon so fresh it squeaked. The guys talking on their CB's reminded her of the boys she had yearned to play with in her youth—the cowboys, Indians, cops and robbers. Now she was allowed to play, but there were still secrets she wasn't supposed to know.

"My deckhand just made us two great tomato sandwiches," a man fishing up by Fort Ross radioed his pal down at Point Reyes. Megan checked the code sheet she had found under a table at the Fisherman's Cafe. "Hey, Captain Frank, 'tomato sandwich' means twenty-five fish."

"He used this super hot sauce," the guy on the radio continued.

"'Hot' means he caught them on the hot pink plugs," she relayed to Frank. At night, in the anchorage, the men bragged about how many "wine coolers" they had drunk. Before Megan knew a wine cooler was fifty fish, she thought the fishermen were all out there getting plastered. There were special groups, some bonded by blood, or by ports, who exchanged code sheets to help each other out. No one talked straight. Even the Italians pretended they couldn't speak English. It was like living in a Nancy Drew novel.

A few days before salmon season opened, Frank announced he had sold the boat and gotten a job driving a truck. A small run the previous year and the state's restrictions shortening each season made Frank one of many fishermen who was forced to sell out. Megan was disappointed, but relieved when Chuck, the new owner of Frank's boat, asked if she'd stay on. He was a young guy who had never fished before, and like most newcomers, he saw salmon fishing as quick, easy money.

"Quite a few of these planks are rotten." Megan tapped on each one as she and Chuck went over the boat. "Frank let things slide pretty badly. This battery is ancient and you really need a second bilge pump. This baby's pretty small."

"Hey, I'm ready to fix all this stuff," Chuck grinned. "Just show me some fish. We'll just fish easy until I get some cash."

The season opened each year in mid-April. Predictably, the ferocious winds arrived with it, keeping the fleet in port. Frustration and anxiety showed on every face while the weather reminded them it had no master. Finally, a promising weather report brought the familiar early morning roar of engines throughout the marina.

"Where we going, Captain?" Megan asked as Chuck powered out the channel one morning, fighting the wake of the larger boats.

"I heard some boats got some big fish out at Cordell Banks yesterday."

"The Banks? That's three hours straight out. This boat isn't exactly, well, you know, in great shape."

"Well, it'll never improve if we don't catch some fish. Look at this weather. It's flat calm, not a breath of wind. We'll be okay."

"Flat calm can change real quick, but I guess you know that." She didn't want to call him ignorant, but the Pacific was known for its dramatic weather changes.

"Hey, I said we're going to the Banks and in case you didn't know, there's only one captain on this boat." Megan's stomach began to knot, sensing a darker side to her new captain.

A horizon dotted with flashes of silver greeted their arrival when they reached the fleet.

"Get the lines in, quick. This is what we've been waiting for. Hurry up, hurry up." The salmon hit the lines the minute Megan lowered them in. Big kings, ten to fifteen pound average. She quickly forgot Chuck's hostile tone as they scooped fish after fish onto the boat. It was a payday for everyone, but as evening approached, the winds picked up in what seemed like minutes. The momentum of the swells increased as the sun inched its way towards the sea.

"Chuck, don't you think we should head in? We're the smallest boat out here."

"What did I say earlier about who's captain? It ain't you, babe. Just rebait the lines and make us some money."

Megan was outraged at his stupidity and then at her own, for putting her life in the hands of a novice.

"Hey, Chuck," someone called on the CB. "Better pick up your gear quick and head in."

It was Earl, commonly known as Captain of the Bodega Bay fleet. "It's not going to be pretty out here once the sun sets."

"Those old guys just can't hack it," Chuck laughed.

"Chuck, are you nuts? Those old guys you're referring to have fished all their lives. They know what they're talking about. Let's get the hell out of here."

"Easy for you to say. You didn't shell out your life savings for this boat."

"No, but my life's on this boat and so is yours."

"The sooner you bait those lines and get to work, the sooner we'll go in."

During the next half-hour, the swells grew larger and more furious. There was no pattern to them, they came from everywhere, crashing against each other like a giant washing machine. Getting a fish on board was close to impossible. As darkness approached, Chuck finally agreed to quit. Megan cried from both anger and pain as her already-bruised legs and hips slammed into the unyielding wood while she tried to secure the gear on deck.

At sunset the sea began its dance. Walls of lucid green water lashed out at the boat. White foam and spray covered the decks, pouring into the bilge at a rate faster than the pump could handle. It was no longer their game. The sea had its own rules. It could tease them, toss them, and perhaps, finally, swallow them. The winds increased with the darkness, the swells now three times higher than the boat.

"Shall I call the Coast Guard?" Megan asked hesitantly.

"Are you crazy? Just get out there and bail."

"I'm tying a safety line on first." Megan's eyes swept the wheelhouse for some line, then glanced below, shocked to see their battery now under water. Calling anyone was no longer an option.

"No time for that. Just go," Chuck ordered.

"Hey, asshole, I'm not losing my life because you're in a stupid panic." She found a line and threw it around her waist, her hands shaking as she tried to tie a knot.

"Great, now you can be tied to the boat when it goes down," Chuck shouted as she crawled out to the open cockpit on her knees. It seemed a hopeless battle. Each bucket of water she threw over the side came back tenfold. She thought about her life, the charade she had played, calling herself an existentialist, claiming God was a cop-out. Now she prayed, knowing her need for a higher power had been there long before this storm.

She'd lost all sense of time as she continued to bail in robot fashion. She wished for just one minute that, like Diane, she too could leave her body and hover above the storm. Chuck's knocking on the glass brought her back.

"I can't hold this wheel another second. My back's killing me. You've got to take over." Megan grabbed the wheel. Holding it on course was like trying to steer in cement. If she didn't angle the boat just right into each wave, they would be tossed end-over-end like a toy, and even if she did, one freak wave could end it all.

She had thought about death at sea before. It seemed a tortuous way to go, not dying instantly, but struggling to stay afloat, choking, then freezing, and all the while knowing you were about to die. She had asked other fishermen if they were ever afraid and reluctantly they had all admitted to moments of fear. In turn, they had asked her, "Why aren't you home baking cookies or raising some kids?" How could she explain that it felt more natural to her to be out on the ocean?

Tears and sea water blurred her vision and she blinked hard trying to focus, not daring to take her hands off the wheel.

"Chuck, look," she yelled, staring in disbelief.

"What?"

"The lights, the lights from the bay."

"Oh my God."

"Oh my God is right." The closer they got to land, the more the winds subsided.

"If we sink now we could swim from here," Megan laughed, still not believing they were going to make it. "It's easy steering now." She handed the wheel back to Chuck. She knew he'd be embarrassed if she brought the boat in and, after all, they were alive, that's all that mattered.

When they pulled up to the dock, Diane was waiting to grab the lines.

"We thought you were goners," Diane cried as she jumped down onto the boat to give Megan a big hug.

"I'm going to the bank tomorrow, Diane."

"You're going back out to the Banks?"

"No—bank—money. I'm going to buy us a boat—a solid, safe boat with all the right equipment."

"Sounds good to me. Come on into the Tides and I'll buy you a hot brandy. All the fishermen have been really worried about you."

"Well, you know, I'm going to give everyone of those old salts a big hug. I love them all. I love you. I even love my ex-captain." She gave Chuck a big squeeze.

"That must have been some storm out there, Megan. A real soul bender, I bet?"

"You have sensibility beyond your years, Diane. Say, do you think sometime you could teach me how to leave my body?"

my man

Jane Kennedy Stuppin

my man
his belly unbuttoned
hanging over his swim trunks,
sometimes worn when
painting *en plein air* if the
sun is out, his head hatted
a flap around his neck like
a french lieutenant legionnaire—
a desert soldier,
not a west sonoma county
painter of oaks and rivers, his
colors meandering wide, no streams
or parallel barns, or telephone beams.

my man
his eyes slanted large
as if some tartar horseman
had abducted his ancestral
grandmother waiting in fields
of galicia before the hapsburg
empire marched its prancing horses
over the plowed earth grained
with wheat in summer and
wild flowers every spring.

my man
returning after the sun
goes down with oceans
of brown hills rolling
into the next and scrub
oak in each crease as if some
giant fingers had tucked them
in to keep the body asleep and
round and firm for feet in dreams
to tip-toe across or three rotund
mad-waa-zelles to slide wide down
in slow motion swells that never come
to the bottom where the canvas ends:
a trinity of no repose.

my man
with thumbs for palettes yellowed
and colored as if a defiant fungus had
planted its spore under his nails not
expecting a carpenter to flail away
at lumber for a privy house or any other
practical purpose enjoying the spectacle
of splattered referred paint hiding its source,
his eye, his eye seeing before the brush strokes.

my man
whose double chin
flows over his neck
concealing the swallow of tonight's
chocolate chip cookie washed down
with a sixteen ounce glass of crystal clear
mineral water from nearby calistoga,
no evian from the land of swiss and
jagged pyrenees.

At the Tidepool

Peg Ellingson

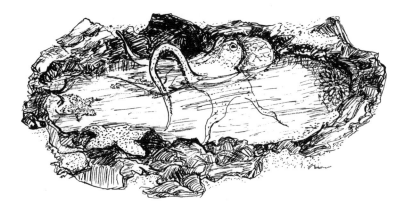

   Paul and Laura hadn't been at their Salt Point campsite
long when the boy, blond and clumsy, appeared to help Paul
raise the tent, handing him the aluminum stakes and moving
out of the way without being told. He talked nonstop in a
loud, earnest voice. In the next ten minutes they learned that
Ian, his mother, and his younger sister occupied Campsite
Seven across the way, that he was eleven and his sister only
four, that they had already explored the tide pools where he
had found a hermit crab named Dennis, and that his father
had left their house last week to live with some woman.
   Ian was worried that his mother hadn't brought enough
wood. Last night's campfire had been fine, but he wasn't sure
they had enough for tonight. He asked if he could do something to earn a few logs, but he wouldn't take any wood for
helping put up the tent because that was before he asked.
   Paul said he couldn't think of any jobs. Her husband liked
children, but Laura could tell he thought Ian was just this side
of being a pest. She said she was going to the little store up the

coast and that Ian could have some wood if he helped her carry supplies from her car to the campsite later. She told him he was lucky to have such a fine campsite next to the ocean. She tried not to sound condescending the way some adults did when they talked to kids.

Ian asked Paul if he wanted to play frisbee. Paul hesitated, but the boy's request was so wistful that Paul capitulated. Laura watched her husband toss the bright orange saucer and the boy's enthusiastic, awkward sprints to catch it. When Ian threw the frisbee it went wild and Paul had to chase it into the line of Monterey pines surrounding the clearing. Finally, Paul stopped the game and waved Ian away. The boy ran across the weedy center of the campground toward his family's round yellow tent under the pines.

As her husband flopped into his canvas chair with a copy of *Seashore Life,* she said, "You're going to make a great father."

"Well, let's hope our kid is more athletic than that one." He smiled, finding his place in the book.

Contrary to her usual impulses, Laura managed to think before she objected to his comment. They were on vacation and she already knew that if she asked Paul what he meant by such a remark, he would sigh and tell her that she was oversensitive about his making a simple observation. She pressed her hands against her belly and glanced across the campground, where Ian's mother was helping her son climb the tree next to their campsite.

Laura didn't get it. How could a man leave his family like that? It didn't matter to her that collapsed families were as common as strong ones these days. A man just couldn't change his mind like that. Now that she was pregnant, it seemed absurd. She thought of Paul's excitement when he saw the baby's heart beating on the sonogram, his pleasure when she had described to him the first flutterings in her womb, like the faintest of winds, like someone's breath on her cheek.

Ian was nowhere in sight when Laura returned from the store, but she had so little to carry it didn't matter. She had bought wood, though, and when it began to grow dark, she suggested they take some of it to Ian's campsite. Paul wanted to shower and unroll the bedding inside the tent before the light faded entirely, so Laura would have to go alone. He reminded her not to stay too long since they planned on waking up for low tide.

Ian's mother was sitting with her arm around him at their campfire. Behind them, the little sister hummed as she washed pine cones in a plastic dishpan then set them in a neat row on the picnic table to dry. A butane lantern had been placed on the table to help her see. Struck by her assured movements, her absorption in the task, Laura thought the little girl didn't seem to mind her father's absence so much. She was with her mother, so she was all right. Then she looked at the way Ian leaned against his mother, the hood of his red sweatshirt pulled tight around his face. It was different for Ian.

"Better hurry, sweetie," the mother called to her daughter. "We're going to have coals soon."

Laura stopped next to the campfire. "I brought some extra wood." She suddenly felt uncertain.

"I'm sorry I didn't come." The boy looked up at her. "We were playing until dinner. Anyway, we do have enough logs for marshmallows."

"Doesn't matter a bit," Laura replied. "But I'll leave these here just in case." She placed the logs next to the campfire.

Ian said to his mother, "I was going to help her carry groceries."

"Ah." The woman looked up. "Ian the worrier. Thanks, but I actually think I brought enough to last. These two will fade pretty quickly, once they have their marshmallows and sing their songs." She smiled and drew her arm tighter around her son. "Which we will do as soon as all of the pine cone babies have their baths."

Ian said, "Mom, she's married to Paul, the one I was playing frisbee with. He's nice, like Dad."

"He's dependable too," Laura blurted. She felt her face go hot.

"Well, that's important, to be dependable," the woman replied, as though she were talking about the weather. Then her voice changed slightly. "And nice. That's important too." She spoke without sarcasm but with amusement. A private joke, perhaps.

"Would you like a marshmallow?" Ian asked Laura, pointing at the peeled sticks propped by the fire. "You can stay and sing with us. Paul can come, too."

"That sounds like fun, but Paul and I want to get up early and explore while the tide is out."

"You'll see those big anemones and sea stars, the yellow ones, if you go early enough," the woman said. For a few minutes they talked about tide pools.

"Tell Paul goodnight for me," Ian said as Laura turned to go.

"Thanks again for the wood," the woman said. "And tell your husband thanks for playing frisbee with Ian."

On her way to their tent, Laura looked back at Ian's campsite and his mother piling the extra logs on their fire. The campground was completely dark except for five or six luminous blurs. She tried to imagine the feelings of Ian's mother, alone now in the world, building up her fire, drawing her children close in the night.

She suddenly felt as though all of them had been flung back into the ancient past. The small fires in the night belonged to a primitive tribe in a strange land, surrounded by unseen dangers. Standing still, she looked up, searching the sky for the familiar constellations, the fixed stars. There they were, where they belonged, like her baby in its warm world, like her husband waiting for her in their little tent.

The next morning, as she and Paul took the trail through the pines to the ocean, she realized Ian and his family would be gone before they returned from the tide pools. As they passed their silent tent, she thought of the little family inside and wished she had stayed to sing at the campfire.

Laura and Paul clambered over the massive rocks on the shore to the outcrops that spilled into the Pacific. Here the waves surged in and out, pouring into countless crevices, creating new worlds with each breath of the tide. Abalone hunters bobbed and dove beyond the surf, searching the underwater reefs. The tide had already covered the larger anemones and sea stars, but snails and purple urchins crowded the visible pools, and crabs scrambled for niches in the sandy confusion of receding waves. Orange bat stars and barnacles clung in abundance to the wet rocks. The first time Laura noticed a hermit crab, she said to Paul, "Oh, look, I wonder if that's Dennis?"

"Dennis?"

"You know, Ian's buddy, the one he told us about."

"Oh, yeah," Paul said. "But according to my seashore book its real name is Pagurus."

"That's not real, it's the name of a species or something, Paul." Then Paul asked why she was so crabby and she had to laugh.

In the afternoon, she found an octopus trapped in a quiet pool, forsaken by the open sea until high tide rose over the rocks. An abalone diver who had surfaced with his catch heard her calling to Paul and swam to the rocks leading to the pool. He stepped along them in his flippers until he arrived at the pool, just as Paul reached the large rock where Laura stood. The diver leaned down and picked up the creature. It squirmed shiny red, translucent against the bright blue bowl of sky.

Laura asked if that was the normal color for an octopus.

"Nah," the diver said. "The ones around here are brown. This one is sick, or maybe he's just pissed off." He cleared his nose and spat into the sea. Water dripped from his hair and rolled down his black wetsuit. The octopus waved its tentacles in all directions.

She became anxious. "Can it breathe?"

The diver shook his head. "Of course not!"

"Then please put it back in the water."

He shot Laura a surprised look, then replaced it in the tide pool. "This your wife?" he asked Paul, who nodded. The diver said to him, "If you don't care, I'll take him home to show my kids."

A strange silence followed. Laura wanted Paul to insist they leave the octopus alone, but he said nothing. Beyond the pool the ocean glittered and thumped. The three of them stood as if suspended in an invisible snare. Laura's chest tightened. If Paul didn't speak, something important would be altered, some irretrievable chance or moment would be lost and nothing would ever be the same.

A large man appeared suddenly from the sea beyond the line of rocks. He lifted his mask back on his head as a wave foamed in and swirled around his waist, then pulled himself up on the rocks next to the first diver and looked in the tide pool. "Oh ho, octopus," he observed.

"I thought I'd bag him up to show the boys," said the first diver. "You ready to go? We've got our limit." He pointed to the abalone bag he had tossed onto dry shore rocks.

The second diver looked up and met Laura's eyes. "You find him?"

"He did," said the first diver, aiming his thumb at Paul.

"I did," Laura corrected.

"She did," Paul agreed.

"Then he's yours," the large man said to her. "It's the law of the sea."

"I want it to go back where it came from." Laura looked at the octopus at the bottom of its rock prison. "Why is it red? Is it sick?"

"No. It's probably scared. They like dark places and there's no place here for an octopus to hide. You don't usually see one this close in." When he looked at her, Laura felt he understood her distress completely.

"Want me to take him back? I'll let go of him out by those rocks." He pointed beyond the surf, where the sun flashed blinding disks off the water.

She nodded and he lifted the octopus from the pool. "C'mon, big fella, I'll take you home."

The first diver said nothing. He stood in the noisy sunlight and gazed at his buddy snorkeling out with the octopus, then scrambled up to the abalone bag, and started inland. Out in the ocean, the second diver reached the rocks beyond the breakwater, then signaled success with his empty hands before starting back to shore. When he emerged down the coast, Laura thought about calling out to thank him, but stayed quiet.

She was trying to make sense of what had happened, but it was as though something had erased her memory. It was the strangest thing. She could clearly imagine the octopus safe in its dark cave beneath the sea. But when she tried to recall what had just happened at the tide pool—the words and expressions, who had said or done what—other thoughts interfered, like the sonogram image of their unborn child and its pulsing heart, or the way the wind carried the faint sounds of Ian's family across the campground last night. Lying in the darkness next to Paul, she had strained to identify the songs, some of them familiar from her own childhood. They had sung so quietly.

Misery swelled in her throat. Laura realized she was waiting for Paul to say something. For a long time they sat side by side on rocks above the tide pools and stared silently out to sea. Beyond the pools, groves of sea palms glistened in the sun then disappeared, swallowed by the incoming surf. Then they appeared again, swaying in the water, nodding shoreward, as though trying to tell her something. The sight of them made her queasy. But high tide was coming in. Soon their gleaming heads would be completely submerged.

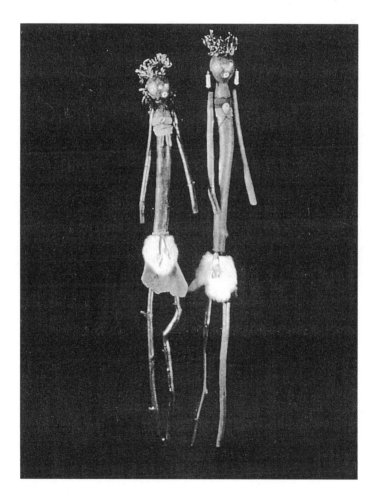

Going to the Where?

Bobby Markels

I haven't been anywhere for a while and I am wondering
where to go for the day, just a good old summer Mendocino
day. Should I drive up through the redwoods, to Eureka, out to
Orrs, down the coast?

We need an adventure, I say to my friend, Judith. Let's go
somewhere.

The Conservancy, she says, you said it was so nice, we can
swim.

I say yeah but I don't remember. It was on the Branscomb
Road I think, I mean I see it, I see this turn, but—I call the
friend I went with last year. It's off the Branscomb Road, she
says, about nine miles, we got to a place and we said, oh this is
easy, and we turned left, something about that bridge right
there but not that obvious. There's sort of a sign, don't you
remember, a sign on the other side, something like that.

I say, no I don't remember but I will when I get there.

So we get in the car. We drive past Fort Bragg; houses are
getting funkier, there are dogs on the road, old trucks appear
and hunchbacked hills, the ocean's far down and a huge bright
gray sky above. I jump out at the Westport store. First I grab a
Hershey bar and two doughnuts—hey, I'm on vacation. And a
diet Coke *with* caffeine. Do you know the way to the Conservancy, I mean how far up Branscomb? Two guys wearing dusty
jeans and worn flannel shirts look at each other. They are very
big from the belt up: big in the chest, lots of bulging pockets,
vests, big hats, lots of testosterone.

It's ah, up the Branscomb Road, about nine miles,
yeah, you just turn, there's a turn, yeah its right on the right.

No, the left, what're you telling her it's the right for, it's the left, it's right there on the left, about ten miles up, you'll see it, you'll know it. So, I'm back in the car, we're buzzing along and then we're on the Branscomb Road.

Oh the feeling of back roads in northern California—the puzzled queries of here it is, not quite here but we're almost there. Didn't we pass this house last year, this bridge, this barn, this weird-shaped tree? Aren't we almost? No, we went to the right, we went to the left, down that road, up that hill, past that stream. There was a white house like that, no a log, a painted white log, no they had a white dog, no a black dog in a white doghouse. There was a grove of trees, like this eucalyptus. No it was fir, you went around and under this sort of grove, a heavy grove, no it was more like a —. It wasn't trees. It was sort of a tunnel. It was a big tunnel, no, that was coming into San Francisco, oh shit.

The mystery, the wonder, the miracle of back roads. I remember what it was, I say: you make a turn but it wasn't exactly where you thought you make a turn, it was a little different. Now here's the nine-mile marker. So you'd think you'd turn left up the road right here at this bridge, but that's too obvious, remember she said it wasn't obvious. So we keep going. We pass a couple of roads on the left. That's not it. This one either. This is it. Yeah, this is it, I remember. And we're ambling along this road the county road turns into, and then another and another, from hard to soft to a narrow strip with hardly enough room for one car, and we're flowing into that slanting, sloping, pastoral land deep into the dark green heart of the northern California back roads.

This might be right. I look at Judith. I kind of remember this turn. (There's a house with lots of trucks and cars, a big barrel, a huge TV antenna, a gray fence.) I say, there was a place sort of like this, yeah we're going right, I remember this long space of cows and sheep and —. It's the wrong road. I know it's the wrong road. On either side with lazy spaces between there are small houses, trucks, trailers, sheep, kids, and cars but its the wrong sheep, the wrong cows, the wrong houses, and we are the wrong people to be here at this time. This isn't it, I say. Are you sure? Judith asks. I know. I mean it looked like this, but this isn't it. Oh my God, I do remember a slant to the right like this and a kind of fork like this and a bunch of little houses like a kind of a community like this, but there were more of them or something. Now this looks like one big place and look—an airstrip. I don't remember an airstrip but there's a fence and there's the sign. Sure, see, it's the same kind of sign like don't come in here or we'll bomb your ass. Okay, it may not be the exact words but that's what they mean. We go around the airstrip. There is a nice house on the right with a big garden and lots of space around it. We stop the car and get out. We are at the beginning of a forest. It is almost dark and in a second we have gone from sunlight to dark damp woods. I feel like I am in the forest primeval. We are on the edge of a burned-out camp—criss-crossed logs, two-by-fours, half-burned out long wood tables, the remains of a dilapidated house or maybe lodge with half the walls gone, a hanging roof with tin patches and big holes of sky showing, garbage cans, and wilted looking outhouses—a deserted, destroyed encampment of some kind. We stand staring. A woman is coming out of the yard by the house, we turn towards her away from the wood towards the sun. Can I help you? I look at her, the garden, the landing field. Something is not quite right. I say we are looking for the Conservancy.

She smiles and says, oh, take this road back, then by the bridge you turn right, you should have turned left when you drove by the bridge. She is wearing shorts and a halter. She looks too pretty, too young, too lively, too cute to live here in this little old family house, too sophisticated, too—. She looks like a gang moll. She looks like Lauren Bacall. We get in the car. I'll tell you, I say, if they were really rich they'd fix up their house but if they're not rich why—how come they have an airstrip? So they must have a plane so they must be rich. They're some kind of officials and they're into graft, something. They're whitewashing money, tax dollars, her husband is a petty official. There's no doubt, I say, something's going on. It's all so quiet, the trees looming up, the dark woods behind us, the happy little house and garden and airstrip and I know that Humphrey Bogart, Sidney Greenstreet, and Peter Lorre are going to land any minute on that airstrip and stay for the weekend.

I know. I've been on California back roads. I've hit places—a tiny hamlet, a crossroads and a restaurant from the twenties—nothing but that one restaurant and one house. Something's going on. And by the ocean, a bar and grille, five houses, a wharf and two boats—what's going on? I am flooded with the mystery of California's past, pirates docking in the fog—dope? what?—and far back into the dusty pink center of a dry desert, two blocks of houses and one gas pump that stands wearily like an old Confederate soldier saluting the California sun. A town so intermingled and interbred so far back that everyone's married their own grandfathers. I've driven into tiny villages, a post office inside a small grocery store the only sign of habitation, and in the weary afternoon dust, three guys sitting on the small step look up at me from crafty, narrowed, back-roads eyes, and I wouldn't get out of my car if you paid me a million bucks. Something's going on.

We drive back to the bridge where I said it can't be that road, that's too obvious, and we make the right turn. Back again into the dry grayish dust of the road and the whispering melting shapes in the distance. Hills like bears, like antelopes, green feathery light coming through easy trees and weathered fences, cows snoozing, goats grazing. We bump bump along, this can't be right. Yes it is, I remember, I mean I really remember, this was the turn. Remember when I said where's that turn and here's the grove of trees, and it's eucalyptus—I told you there was a grove of trees like a tunnel—isn't this like a tunnel, a sort of tunnel? That mail box, I remember that mailbox. We've got it, I knew it. When we made that turn, when we saw that lane, when we crossed that creek, when we saw that dog. That's the dog! It's the same dog—and here's the sign, the sign on the right, on the tree, I told you. Where? Judith asks. Here, here. Judith's like, where? What? Are we here? I'm shouting, here's the sign, there's the river, you go through that fence, the one that says don't go through. She's still like, what where? Oz, I shout, Oz. The wonderful city of Oz. We're here, we've arrived, thank you God, lordy, lordy, we are saved, we've found the California Nature Conservancy.

We stay for a few hours, we swim, we lie on rocks, we soak in sun, we walk through trees, but all that's for another story.

We are happy, fulfilled, spent, exhausted, and as we start to drive back past the little houses and now familiar twists and turns, the light is pouring into us, the sun is pouring into us, the trees, grass, pastoral hills are filling us up, flushing us out, through our skin, our bones, our marrow and muscle, down to our skeletons we are flushed with the glory of this north country, this California. The dirt road smooths into gravel and then cement, we pick up speed, and then I spot far ahead the cross at Route One. Suddenly the air is cooler. There is the cold gray light of the coast and the salt smell of ocean. A huge sky appears. Everything is recalled. It is almost dusk. I put my coat on over my shoulder and even though we've been driving my '94 Thunderbird, as I stop to put my arms into my jacket, I feel like I'm on the last lap of a long buggy ride, about to say giddiap to my tired old horse.

Light

Joanne Surasky

Icy water forced itself into every opening of Emery's entire body. This was not like the terrifying time he jumped off the high dive when he was ten. This was pure evil, something personal, something reaching out of the night to get him.

He couldn't breathe. He didn't know how deep he was. Something was holding him down. He'd been able to kick out the glass and slither through the window when a goddamn torn-loose tree racing down the stream in his direction shoved his truck off the bridge. The truck slowly went over the edge, nose first.

Emery knew driving across his old bridge, already under several inches of water, would be tricky. But he couldn't have predicted this. Las Piedras stream, brought to life with the rains, had been making a roaring noise all day and the noise got louder as the storm got worse. Rain saturated Joline's garden, water sheeted off their roof, leaping out over the shiny new gutters he'd just put up. Boiling rivulets of coffee-colored foam turned the stream from a slow, pastoral watercourse to a tumbling, destructive spillway—digging trenches around hills, cutting across the slant of sheep pastures and pouring silt into the ocean estuary, where seals bred.

Eight inches of rain in an hour-and-a-half the TV had said.

The bridge had no sides, and the worn-down wood felt slick and unsure under his tires. He'd made it about halfway across when the tree slammed the bridge, its branches closing around the truck like a fist. "I don't believe this," he'd said. He thought he'd gun the motor and keep going, but the tree held the truck and pushed like it had a job to do. A branch cracked his windshield and jammed against the driver's door. Emery's truck finally gave up, eased sideways, and dropped down into the churning waters.

About dusk Emery had put on his long yellow slicker to walk the pasture that held the new lambs. They had their mothers; there was feed. They had their lean-to on high ground; everything seemed under control. He'd come back tired and wet and sat down to corned beef hash and eggs when a couple of big gusts shook the house and the electricity went out. The six o'clock news cut off with a dizzy little hiss. Except for the glow of the wood stove, the room was pitch black. Probably another waterlogged eucalyptus downed the line. It happened a lot in the wind and rain, and it drove Joline crazy.

She started in on him about the flashlight batteries. He'd forgotten to buy new ones at the hardware. Now with the electricity off she shook the flashlights at him, one in each hand, showing him how they were turning orange and dim, yelling about how she couldn't feed the kids in the dark. Then she said, "Where are the candles I asked you to bring? Where are they? Shit, Emery, you can't hold a thought in your head more than five minutes."

He couldn't fight with words, he couldn't grab them out of the air like Joline did—words that cut like kitchen knives or beat on his head like an iron skillet. He had to get out of there—maybe go down to Four Corners Tavern, see if they had electricity, maybe get up a game with somebody.

Emery rose from the table, took one of Joline's flashlights, felt around in the kitchen drawer, found five candle stubs, and melted the bottoms with a match so they'd stick in some plastic cups. Then he lit them, placed them at even intervals on the table so they made the kids' eyes shine, sat down again, and finished eating, wiped up the egg yolk with his bread, put his dishes in the sink, walked over to the coat hooks, shrugged on his slicker, and went out the front door.

Joline stood there, watching his every move. For once she didn't say anything, like, "You can't just leave us in the dark." Words could pull him back from things he wanted to do. He was a grown man, for Christ's sake. He could feel her anger— steely and self-righteous.

Emery tried to give the door a good hard slam but five days of rain had swelled the wood, and it closed after him with a flat thud. The last thing he saw before going out the door was the kids, smeary with peanut butter and milk, sitting in a row at the table watching him with their big eyes.

The dogs hadn't come skidding around the house like they usually did to try for a ride. They weren't stupid. He had to make a run for the shelter of his truck. Even the cab door was too wet to slam.

His headlights in the rain shone like dull animal eyes. Once he got across the bridge and down to the paved road, he'd head for the tavern. There'd sure to be a bunch of old boys who needed to get out—just like him. Four Corners usually had their electric when most people didn't.

Someday he planned to go to the electric company and complain. Service always came last to Emery's place. You could drive around and see lights in the other farms and you knew they had their electricity. That really aggravated Joline.

When they courted and he'd shown Joline his property, left to him by his Granddad, she'd called it a paradise. Sweet spring flowers bloomed, the wild iris, the big yellow lupine—showing off all over the place—and the little blue lupine. She'd noticed the way golden poppies furled into tight orange roses before the sun forced them open. Clear, rich green pastures, kept neat as a park by grazing sheep, surrounded the farm buildings. The house needed fixing but it had a porch around two sides, and three bedrooms. He'd asked her to marry him as they stood on the wisteria-draped porch while fog rolled in from the west, bringing the smell of sea spray.

Emery had no feel for how far under water he was. He expected his heart to stop from the cold. His head buzzed and brilliant flashes of light splintered into pieces behind his eyes. Is this how dying feels? He wondered if Granddad would come out of the light to meet him, show him around like that plea-surable day Emery joined the Grange.

The buzzing quit when a thought tempted him: "Why not give up?" Why struggle? His panic evaporated and he floated lazily, no need to breathe. Suddenly he was warm. Remaining fragments of light began to form a picture. Bright sun. Blue sky, clouds racing by—making rapid light and shadow patterns, like movies that speed up time. An image came into sharp focus. He heard singing and organ music. People he knew stood in front of the local church. It looked like Granddad's funeral.

"It's your funeral, boy," a voice said. "Not mine."

Joline wore a sleek black dress. She'd dressed the kids in white—two girls and a feisty baby boy—little angels.

Folks huddled together and talked about Emery.

"For a college boy, he handled that farm pretty well. Learned all there is to know from his grandfather," a neighbor said.

"Temper got him into trouble, though," the neighbor's wife said with a prissy mouth. "That's why he drowned."

The view changed.

"So, Joline, dear, will you stay on?" the pastor's wife asked.

Joline hugged the baby and the girls hung onto her dress. "No, I'm going back to my parents' place."

The scene shifted quickly to a familiar street of faded California bungalows. Joline's family's house. Orange trees and an RV filled the front yard; goats and chickens were penned up in back. He never liked that neighborhood, hot and dusty in the summer with all those trashy oleanders in loud pinks and reds. He saw Joline in shorts and a halter, gossiping with her girlfriends, everybody's kids riding cheap plastic tricycles up and down the sidewalk.

Back to the church. A woman in white orthopedic shoes spoke with certainty to her husband. "A girl that pretty won't have trouble marrying again. Just go for some courses at the junior college and grab herself a new man to take over the farm."

The husband said, "Shame Emery drowned right on his own property. Drinking, most likely."

"I wasn't drinking, you old toad," Emery wanted to shout.

Another shift, and he saw Joline's tall, new husband wearing a gray Stetson, walking the fence lines on Emery's property. "Thinks he's a rancher with that hat on. Christ, there's my dogs, followin' right in his footsteps."

With a vicious jolt, the picture went dark. Emery, still under water, still holding his breath, had lost all feeling in his arms and legs. Those things he'd just seen and heard had taken a split second. Time had returned to real time, and his lungs felt like they'd burst. Seething anger welled up in Emery. He wasn't going to let some guy walk off with his wife, his kids, his farm—even his dogs. He would break away from whatever wrapped itself around him. He was going home.

He gathered the strength he had left and thrashed like he'd gone mad: kicking, straining, twisting. Finally he felt something give way. Damn. Now he knew. All this time he'd been held by his fucking yellow slicker, caught in the branches of that damn tree. He'd managed to rip it just in time. He could no longer hold his breath. Emery slid from his torn-apart coat like a snake shedding its skin.

Water continued to scour his raw sinus, his throat, and ears, but Emery didn't care. He'd reached the surface. He desperately sucked air into his lungs.

Shit, he was tired. He'd let the stream carry him for a bit.

As a kid he'd played around the gentle Las Piedras during summers he stayed with his grandparents—swinging on willows, hopping the bleached rocks, disturbing blinking lizards where they baked in the white-hot sun. He'd grown to be a reckless swimmer, had been pounded by ocean surf, and could outswim riptides. In all his years he'd never come this close to drowning.

Darkness. He couldn't see. He thought of Las Piedras' usual path and remembered a wide, rocky stretch at the western edge of his property. He'd try to snag himself on the boulders, pull himself out. When the stream ran full, there were rapids. You could hear them, a sort of rumble.

Emery rushed along, and he heard the deep, vibrating thunder of approaching rapids too soon. Choppy swells surged over him as he smashed against a large rock. He clung to the rock like a starfish and held his head high enough to breathe while the current tried to pry him off. He hoped to God there were other rocks nearby.

He dragged himself from boulder to boulder against the rapids. Should he go over here or over there? He wasn't sure. His sense of direction was gone. He'd lost his boots. He'd torn his skin and fingernails; his bones ached. He almost cried with relief when he smelled earth and his battered fingers sank into the wet clay of the stream bank. Barefoot, coughing water from his lungs, grabbing at reeds and willows, Emery climbed the steep, crumbling bank. Over and over he slid backwards in the mud, but knew he'd make it to the top.

At last, stretched on the grass, he took long ragged breaths. Rain washed the mud from his body. Were those the dogs barking? Would they find him? He'd crawl to the house if he had to.

He loved that house. He thought about it, warm and slightly smoky from the wood stove. The kids snuffling in their sleep, Joline in her flannel robe, dabbing cream on her freckles. If there was electricity, Joline would be in a good mood, might even be glad to see him. He'd tell her what happened and she'd take care of his hurts. She'd be scared when he said he'd thought he was near drowning. She'd put her arms around him and tell him he was okay, he was home.

Was the rain stopping? Emery sat up, blinked, and found he could see his house on top of the hill, way off in the distance, lit like a beacon.

That Joline—she'd turned on every goddamn light, upstairs and down.

He stood shakily, pushed the hair out of his eyes, and set off, barefoot, toward his shining house.

Love from Scotia

Dee Watt

My mother called me her frail child. My father's Sunday snapshots supported her judgment. Every time he brought home a new batch, I saw with my own eyes that I was thin, all arms and legs and skinned knees. But I felt strong. Beginning when I was four-years-old, I invented secret tests to prove my strength. I climbed our grapefruit trees to their highest branches, where I hid in the leaves until I could come down unobserved. I shinnied up old crooked rungs to the top of the water tank. Locking my armpits over the edge, I waited for long minutes until I could see the green-black puddle at the bottom. At that same age, I perfected my escape from the yard. Behind the shed was a coil of rusty barbed wire which I covered with boards so I could scale the fence. Spiders ruled that space, and I whispered, "Please let me pass."

My mother commanded, "Never leave the yard." The spiders were forgiving, but Mom stripped the leaves off jasmine branches and switched me with them when I came home.

Most of the times when my father traveled, my little sister Janna and I stayed with Mom in Taft. He drilled oil wells for the Standard Oil Company all over the West. In his absence, I climbed out of the yard every day into a neighborhood of children who shared their bikes and roller skates with me. Each day I returned to the sharp pain of the jasmine switches. Then, when I was seven, the summer trips began. My father drove us north from the San Joaquin Valley toward Humboldt County. When we got to the Golden Gate Bridge that first summer, my arms began to prickle with the possiblity of an escape. The toll booth was open both directions on the bridge then, and the northbound toll booth began my rite of passage. Somehow, after my father paid for our crossing, I knew we would not turn back.

Though Mom insisted on all windows being closed, the sea wind pushed damp salty air through the cracks. On the bay, it churned the ripples into white spray and blew the sailboats sideways. Everything was in motion. Not even becoming carsick the minute we hit the twisty old Redwood Highway could ruin my pleasure. The giant redwoods soared into the sky on all sides.

My mother's last big scene for the whole two weeks was to coerce my father, who loved respectability, into the rattiest motel she could find. My sister and I begged for a place with a swimming pool. Then my dad quietly tried for someplace decent, but our driving day never ended until we were all too exhausted to argue with her any more.

Despite my mother's unwavering control over where we stayed, I began each of those drives away from the desert fantasizing that we would stop at a motel with a pool. I craved water in any form. The puddle at the bottom of the old tank, bathtubs, sprinklers, I loved them all, but my love for swimming pools was passionate. Close at hand, however, pools terrified me. Mom's gruesome tales of death by drowning couldn't squelch my longing, but they clamped my hands to the pool gutters. Even surrounded by the beloved smell of chlorine, I could not force my nose into the water.

My father's family was all in northern California. His sister, my Aunt Frances, lived with her husband and our older cousins in Scotia. The summertime Eel River ran through the trees in warm swift curves until it sprawled out into the Pacific Ocean. My aunt took us to sheltered places to splash and wade.

With all that natural water and my Aunt Frances to guide me, those vacations showed me happiness without worry. My aunt offered an orderly and comfortable household, casually preparing meals of fried chicken and native berry pies. Her kitchen always smelled delicious. My mother hated to cook, but she loved to sit at the dinner table listing everyone's efforts to ruin her life. At my aunt's house she was silent, her face an unfamiliar mask. Aunt Frances never knew how she pulled our hair in secret or called us names that we struggled to disbelieve.

In the wooded hillsides behind Scotia, Janna and I picked huckleberries and thimble berries for dessert. Every single twiggy pail of squashed fruit became a scrumptious pie. We scratched our legs on brambled hillsides searching for the biggest and the best. We scorned the common blackberries. When we were tired, we lay on our backs to watch the crows scold in and out of the redwood canopy. Once, as a black garden snake slipped across Janna's leg, I ordered her to freeze until he went on his way. Poor Janna. I only tolerated her company. I couldn't run away from Aunt Frances, but asking permission for each outing meant taking four-year-old Janna with me. My sister slowed me down, so I made her suffer snakes and spider webs without sympathy. I wanted her to be tough. Though we came home dirty and ravenous, dinner always waited, and the conversation was easy. I didn't shrink away if Aunt Frances hugged me goodnight.

My aunt, the redwoods, the Eel River, and the wild Pacific made up heaven for me. I slid my hands and forearms onto the trunks of the huge first-growth trees, leaning all my weight into their roughness. Much of the logging that restored San Francisco after the quake of 1906 was done further south, so Humboldt County in the 1940s had ancient groves. I was mesmerized by the intricate lines of ferns that seemed to float in the deep shade. I picked out the most fragile threads of trails, slipping through, fronds brushing up to my hips. The forest was my refuge.

At the river, I huddled in the rocky sand, hot and scared, while other kids played in the water. It moved fast. There were no pool gutters. Finally, sweaty and disgusted by my own fear, I inched into the Eel. I braked after each step, but at last the water jiggled just over my collarbones. The river cooled me. I relaxed, rocking forward and pushing back against the current. I even allowed it to carry me a few feet downriver. My arms windmilled in front of me, and my chin pointed skyward.

At last I was able to flounder and dog paddle all the way across. My belly jumped with excitement as I did it over and over and over. I wouldn't leave that river. When finally I shivered onto the blankets, blue in the lips, Aunt Frances wrapped me up in towels and praise. I heard my mother say, "You are such a disgusting girl. You never know when to stop. Now you will be sick all day tomorrow." But my aunt had begun rubbing my hair, so my mother's words couldn't come too near. A few minutes later, Aunt Frances bent over to check on me. Her hair in the sun was a shimmering halo around her face. I was healthy the next day. I was strong.

We all drove over to the Mendocino Coast where my aunt and my father had grown up in Little River. Daddy showed Janna and me the houses his father and grandfather had built and the beach with big boulders where he had gathered abalone. His oldest brother, killed in a logging accident, was buried in the Little River cemetery. I always begged to go there so I could see our name in stone. I sat on the rocks bordering the family plot, my bare feet on grass that was mine. After two weeks we drove home to Taft, and all that I had learned about joy evaporated. As my stomach lurched on the curves I closed my eyes to the big trees, and the Golden Gate crossing felt sad and dull. When my father left for work on Monday morning, my mother began. She talked about how stupid Grandma Annie had been to raise her children out on that remote northern coast. "Look what happened," she said. "One of them dead young. None of the others even civilized."

She took Janna and me into the front yard to pick up trash scattered on the parched Bermuda grass. She showed us that being away always made a mess at home, and then she went on, "Your Aunt Frances is the worst of the lot. She put you in so much danger every day that I didn't sleep a wink the whole time. That was no vacation for me, I'll tell you." I squinted at my mother's narrow mouth. I watched as she claimed to love her daughters more than life.

Then the neighbor turned on his sprinklers. As the spray glinted in the light behind Mom, I remembered Aunt Frances looking down at me on the blanket by the river. How her sun-drenched hair gleamed. I had goosebumps from loving her. Over her head I saw again the line of deepest blue where the tops of the big trees met the sky. The boundaries of my life were in that faraway line, shining invitation.

Bon Ami, Mon Amour

Christy Wagner

Loreen Lorenz, a dishwater blond and genius mother of two, worked long hours. She commuted forty miles from Mendocino to work at the Mutt Hut restaurant in Ukiah. In between commutes, she wrote inspirational tracts for religious greeting cards to pick up a little extra money to help finance her son's college applications.

Bo Lorenz, her son, was an exceptional young man and deserved the best in life as did her brilliant daughter, Raquel Lorenz. What a fine trio they were: Loreen, Bo, and Raquel. Unfortunately, checks were bouncing, the car needed new tires and brakes, and the electric bill kept going up with the long hours the children spent in the hot tub.

The main problem with the Mutt Hut, besides its location, was that the average entree was $5.95, which meant tips were small. However, Loreen was new at waitressing and she couldn't yet afford to be picky. She was intentionally collecting experience and honing her innate abilities to the point where everyone would recognize exactly what she had to offer.

"Loreen Lorenz," her Tai Chi instructor, Pheelo Lovestead, used to whisper at dawn on Saturday mornings at Heeser Park, "you have a lot to offer. Believe in yourself, Loreen. You can do anything! I see your inner light."

Indeed, Loreen picked up Tai Chi exceptionally fast and worked it into her waitressing routine, quickly impressing her unique style into the minds of her customers.

"There's something about the way you slide a plate onto the table, Loreen," commented Billy Joe Applewood, "that makes me feel good. I believe you actually improve my digestion."

"I'm so glad to hear that, Billy Joe. The better you digest, the more creative you can be. I visualize a world where—what are you staring at?"

"Could you move like that again, Loreen? It's so pretty the way you slice your hands through the air. Gosh you people from the coast do things different."

"Yes, Billy Joe, I can. See? It's easy and effortless for me. That's how all life should be. I know in my heart it's possible."

The next Saturday morning, Loreen Lorenz was five minutes late for her Tai Chi lesson. Heeser Park was dense with fog and the rising sun was invisible. She wandered for five minutes more before Pheelo Lovestead stepped into her path, almost tripping her.

"Here you are, Loreen Lorenz," he murmured. "Let's get to work. Where did we leave off? Oh, yeah, your mom was wrong about you. Your dad was wrong about you. They said you would never amount to anything. So were your ex-husbands. They were wrong when they said you threw away five perfectly good men. Move your foot like this."

"Actually there were only four," corrected Loreen as she followed Pheelo, gliding around in the fog soup, executing precise movements. He ignored her and continued murmuring modulations of personal reassurance. This was part of his unique recuperative technique for enhancing students of Tai Chi. He intended his voice to enter her unconscious brain and create change.

Listening to him, Loreen was reminded of someone from her childhood, someone very kind. "Pheelo's hair is like Jesus' with a little bald spot in place of the halo," she told Raquel in the kitchen later. "Plus, he moves like Howdy Doody. He's got those same loose legs, the same shoulder slump, the same freckly grin. He sees my innate qualities shining through just like Howdy would if he were real."

"Great, Mom, but why are his pants so tight?"

"In the fog his voice sounds just like Big River lapping on the shore. He's a natural instructor, dear." Loreen pushed her dishwater hair behind her ears and wiped away tears with the back of her hand. She was chopping onions for the school potluck.

"Did Howdy's pants fit like that?"

"Don't make fun. Look how fast I'm progressing." As she spoke, Loreen spun and sliced the air with great fervor although it was 7:00 a.m. on a Wednesday morning. "See how effortless it is?"

When Bo came home and announced that Pheelo was opening the Bon Ami Cafe, complete with a local-habitat flower garden at the corner of Covelo and Kasten in Mendocino, Loreen said, "I wonder why he didn't mention it?"

"Mom, you won't have to drive so far!" squeaked Raquel, her mouth full of banana. "Pheelo will hire you for sure. He sees your innate qualities shining through."

"Zimmy Limwood is working for him already," said Bo. "She's only in high school. Without any experience, she's gonna make twice what you make at the Mutt Hut. You'd better apply quick."

"The kids in the kitchen will have to interview you," warned Pheelo, hemming and hawing when Loreen asked him about his restaurant. She suddenly remembered him cautioning her, "You'll never find a waitressing job locally. Nobody's leaving. Nothing is changing." It had seemed an odd statement at the time. Things always change. Of all people, a Tai Chi instructor should know that.

"You haven't witnessed my special style of serving," she replied, her eyes sparkling with the thought of demonstrating her own special style to an artist and free spirit like Pheelo Lovestead.

Pheelo's demeanor changed. He ruffled like a rooster and began pacing as if he were wearing spurs.

"Incidentally, I've raised my Tai Chi rates," he said. "I feel you've been taking advantage of me, Loreen Lorenz. You don't pay me what everybody else does."

"I'm sorry, Pheelo. What would you like me to pay? Pheelo?"

He stopped and stared Loreen in the eyes, as if he were really seeing her for the first time.

"I won't decide. The kids in the kitchen will decide. We're that kind of place. Nouvelle cuisine. Special aura. We only need one more person, no more, no less. Here's my address. We'll interview you tomorrow at 4:00 p.m. sharp."

"He's not going to hire me," thought Loreen Lorenz. She shivered and reminded herself that attitude was everything. "Stop being defeatist," she scolded herself. "Like Pheelo says, you can do it." And she practiced her serves while commuting to work.

The next day Loreen had the 8:00 a.m. to 4:00 p.m. shift at the Mutt Hut. She arranged to leave work early and drove an hour and fifteen minutes to her job interview, wearing a nearly new dress and eating her sprout sandwich en route. She tried a few of the more difficult Tai Chi moves on the road and was satisfied she was in fine form for the interview in spite of being exhausted and so broke she had to count change for gas.

Walking into the Bon Ami Cafe at exactly 4:00 p.m., she admired the local-habitat garden which was full of pink and blue flowers and sage and parsley and rosemary. She found Pheelo inside surrounded by the seraphim and cherubim who formed his staff.

"Come this way," he instructed her as he entered a small office next to the kitchen. He closed the door and they sat down on plaid chairs. Pheelo had a strange look on his face as if he had swallowed a fish hook.

"What was your name?" he asked.

Impatient to demonstrate her serves, Loreen Lorenz shifted on the plaid chair, and waited for Pheelo to ask her the right questions.

"What did you say?"

"Nervous?" he grinned impersonally.

Was this man really her Tai Chi instructor? She leaned forward and scrutinized him. Maybe she should have run around the block before she came inside after all that driving.

"So, Loreen, tell me. What would you serve?" he asked. "What do you have planned for Friday night, the fifteenth of March?"

"Pardon?"

"Oh, no ideas? None at all?"

"I'd show them a menu. Or, do you do it improv here?" This was not going the way Loreen Lorenz had planned. She should be flying through the air with resolute slices and salutes, not sitting on this squeaky plaid chair on rollers, her face squinched quizzically in Pheelo Lovestead's direction. What was he asking? By the end of the interview, she still didn't know.

He told her the next day that he'd been lucky to find a great guitarist from Sebastopol who was willing to relocate and try waitressing and besides, Zimmy Limwood, his star employee, couldn't work with Loreen Lorenz.

"You're friends with Zimmy's mother. It wouldn't be cool."

Feeling as if she were in India riding an elephant, Loreen Lorenz began to sway. Remembering her bills and her long commute, Loreen began to cry.

She didn't want to. She didn't mean to. It was an old habit. Instead of leaving she asked a question. "I've only been to the Limwood's house twice in ten years. Does it really count?"

Pheelo Lovestead nodded soberly. Maybe she didn't know what he was talking about but she knew what he meant. He meant, no. No. He meant no.

Tai Chi would never be the same. Loreen Lorenz quit her lessons and didn't go back even after she got a better job farther down Kasten Street at the Bonne Vie Restaurant, where her life became as easy and effortless as she had foreseen. She could spin and twirl and slice and chop while serving up magnificent concoctions to big tippers. Eventually Pheelo hired her children, Bo and Raquel, who became very fond of him.

One day much later when they met in the grocery store, Pheelo said to Loreen Lorenz, "That day you left, I went in my office and cried. I knew what it meant to you. I knew what I did to you."

"I had to hurry to work in Ukiah after you told me," confessed Loreen Lorenz. "My eyes were so red that customers asked if I had a sunburn."

"Me, too," said Pheelo Lovestead.

"What?"

"I had to go to work, too. It was really hard."

Loreen learned later that the guitarist Pheelo hired was the niece of his lettuce distributor and that she had broken 1,200 glasses in the first three months, costing Pheelo more than the break he got on lettuce. When the discouraged guitarist returned to Sebastopol, Loreen heard that Zimmy Limwood and the kitchen kids didn't even say goodbye. Furthermore, over the next ten years, Loreen Lorenz was not invited to the Limwood house even once, although she won the waitress of the year award and was featured in a full-page interview in *The Press Democrat* for earning the most tips of any waitress, anywhere, which enabled her to send her kids to Yale and Harvard.

It was Ron at Schlafer's gas station who finally said, "It's not easy to get a job in Mendocino when you're local."

Cows in the Laguna

Karen Eberhardt Shelton

To someone blind
the cows might sound
like small waves brushing sand
in their one body
made of many bodies
following one tide of grass.
But the Laguna is more
than what we suppose
are grass and shoals of mud,
being also the subtle haven
of herons and ducks,
migratory birds that pass
before we knew they had arrived,
sheep at the far edge
and green life under hooves
and webs. The blind
might wonder at the smell,
the swishing, puffs of air
bursting from cow noses
as they sway with one body,
the stamp of weight
crushing from pennyroyal
its scent until it fills
the air, until each gentle
black and white slow beast
and everything else around
is floating in this wild perfume.

Not Our Land

Walking seven miles one polished Saturday
with arms swinging and dog in my left hand
and tee shirt a perfect fit for warm February sun
I hoped for a place along the route
where I could slip in, cavort in the glow of mustard,
walk to the crown of a small hill, look for snails in a creek,
do whatever felt most natural in all that blue air.
Or just ponder a question about the shade of myrtle blooms
and which way the babbling creek runs.
But there is always a fence or gate or something locked
and posted that forbids us to be ourselves wherever
over-zealousness of possession stares down
the sweet taste of countryside inviting visitors
to fling themselves among the wild mushrooms
and calla lilies, giddy and heedless on a mild winter day.

So much for the enforced distance between me and what is
intrinsically neutral; the way land is divided
and made into islands for whoever first comes to it
then wraps it in multiple barriers as if to say
I should never walk barefaced into the blossoms
and madrigals of grass harmonizing with spring,
or watch silent bark holding in the lifeforce of trees
and the way cycles and replenishment are taking place
in the most inconspicuous and modest of living things;
never run in and seize them with my lungs,
let my body billow with knowing them,
embrace their inimitable color and form
like the pagan I am, the wonder-struck grass picker
quivering to push up a sea-green hill and disappear
around the bend of its crown and the undulations beyond.

Instead, I walk by, truculant and yearning,
my good dog beside me also wanting the same break from law,
the pair of us needing to be joined to the world's skin
that shimmers around us, beckons and calls—
all the while denied because we lack ownership.

Apple Harvest in Sebastopol

One early morning on Tilton Road
Mexicans were laughing under the trees
while the sun broke

around the sound of apples thumping
into their buckets,
and several vans came bringing more men
and more laughter and the sound
of more apples thumping crisply
into the buckets.

The men laughed together
and walked all around under the trees
picking apples in the first light
of morning, laughing and milling
with the cold red October apples
rounding into their hands
and down into the buckets
and finally the bins,

laughing as though frost
and the cheeks of apples at daybreak
were pure joy.

Karen Eberhardt Shelton

The Big Apple Splits

Joyce Griffin

The Gravenstein apple tree near the vegetable garden bore a greater abundance of fruit on her branches this year than ever before. She had groaned a bit beneath the weight in early June, but no one in the big house heard. When she spoke to the wind the other day, they decided to make a split.

"I'll go," said the Grav. "You be right behind me." The wind gave a swift shove, splitting Grav's old and worn trunk right down her middle. The western half of her lay low in the garden; the eastern half stood firm. Little green apples tumbled onto the tomatoes and zucchini.

In the past, the master of the ranch had supported the Gravenstein's heavy branches with redwood two-by-fours, trimmed and packed her wounds like a good doctor. But years had gone by without apple mishap and the doctor hadn't expected trouble.

The moan of a chainsaw hacking at the Grav's fallen west side broke the quiet of the tranquil summer afternoon in the garden. The half that had not gone along with the split, the half that still stands laden with fruit, with the wind at her back, sighs, "I'm good for another fifty years."

Gone to Weed

Mary Gaffney

The sale notice had been tacked to the Occidental bulletin board that morning. The McGregors looked at the property before anyone else. The price was right, but the dwelling was a tiny pink mobile home. "I can't live in a pink trailer," said Mrs. McG.

"We could paint it," said Mr. McG, looking beyond the tiny house on wheels to the forest. They saw redwoods, Douglas fir, California bay laurel, madrone, live oak, and black oak. In the foreground, sun shone on Gravenstein apple trees hung with fruit of variegated colors. The two oldest children were already out of the car.

"Go ahead and pick one, kids," said an old man who walked out to meet them. Rafe boosted his younger sister Sunny to help her reach the apples. He picked one for himself, took a bite, and held out the Gravenstein to Mr. McG.

"Dad, it's the best apple I ever tasted."

They bought the place without Mrs. McG ever looking inside the mobile home. Eventually, they'd build a real house. The children could finally have a dog, maybe even a rabbit. They'd plant a big vegetable garden and raise a few farm animals. In 1974 living off the land was a popular concept with people who'd never actually tried it, people like them.

One way Mr. McG intended to live off his land was by growing his own marijuana. That would save him some money, and make him some money. He wouldn't get caught because he would only sell to friends. His friends lived in urban areas where they couldn't risk growing their own.

He emptied his stash into the lid of a shoe box and tilted the lid back and forth until the seeds all rolled loose from the leaf. He put the seeds into an empty film canister. They would be his beginning. He dreamed of running through fields of man-sized plants and woke up smiling. He loved the dream, but he didn't really plant fields of marijuana. He didn't have that much land or that many seeds or that much greed.

The McGregors started building. Sometimes it seemed that the children grew faster than the house, but with family and friends helping, they finally finished their home. Before they knew it, Rafe entered El Molino High School, Sunny started seventh grade, and Toni moved into the second. All those years the vegetable garden had been a family affair, but the marijuana remained Mr. McG's private plot, his hobby, his passion. That fall, Mr. McG lost his privacy.

The sun dropped low in the west, backlighting the red and yellow leaves of the fruit trees. A piliated woodpecker passed overhead with sweeping wingbeats. Toni and Mrs. McG picked lima beans, white corn, and perfectly ripe tomatoes for dinner. Mrs. McG took the vegetables inside. Toni stayed in the garden, working with her dad, until the sun went down and it started to cool off. Then she went inside and helped Rafe and Mrs. McG shell the lima beans, saving the pods for Peter Rabbit.

"I don't even like lima beans," complained Rafe.

"Shuck the corn then," said Mrs. McG.

"Why doesn't Sunny help?"

"She already made an apple pie for dessert, peeled the apples, everything."

"Is it our favorite or some 4-H experiment?" Rafe asked.

"It's our favorite."

They worked silently for a few minutes. The last light of dusk dissolved like a breath. Mrs. McG said, "That crazy Daddy is working out there in the dark."

Toni said, "I'll check on him." She turned on the porch light and stepped out. Before she'd even shut the door, she screamed, "Daddy's hurt! He's yelling."

Rafe raced outside in his stocking feet and Sunny ran into the kitchen.

"You stay here," Mrs. McG said to the girls. "I'll go see if I can help." Rafe and Mr. McG emerged from the woods. "What's going on?" she asked.

"Someone tried to rip us off and would have succeeded if I hadn't been out there. They couldn't see me because of the blackberry bushes between the grass garden and the vegetable garden. I couldn't see them either, but I heard them. I wish I'd been smart enough to sneak up on them, but I was so startled and mad that I screamed, 'I'm gonna get you bastards.' I called for Rafe and ran for the garden gate. They took off, and here we are."

"Did you see who it was?"

"I just saw two guys. I couldn't identify them. Did you see them, Rafe?"

"I didn't even see that much," said Rafe. "It's dark."

"Would someone get a flashlight?" asked Mr. McG.

They were all supposed to keep a flashlight beside their beds in case of earthquake or the regular winter power outages, but each summer the flashlights disappeared or the batteries wore down. Mrs. McG finally found one that worked, and they all went to inspect the grass garden.

Twelve plants had been pulled out of the ground and lay in a neat pile. "They weren't even going to leave me one plant," said Mr. McG. "The bastards were going to wipe me out."

Mrs. McG said, "If you'd found your garden empty, they'd have heard you yell all the way down at the Union Hotel."

"So you were growing..." Sunny looked at her little sister and her voice trailed off. "Did you know about the secret garden?" she asked Rafe.

"Not really."

Mr. McG put one arm around Rafe and the other around Sunny. "I didn't want anyone else in the family to have anything to do with it because it's...well..."

"I know," said Sunny.

Rafe nodded solemnly.

Mr. McG said, "Thanks for coming when I called, Rafe. Are your feet okay?"

"To tell you the truth, I was so pumped up I didn't notice. I just hope Mom won't expect me to get all the burrs out of my socks."

"She won't," said Mom. "We're still lucky. They didn't actually get away with any plants."

"They shouldn't have been harvested at night. They shouldn't have been harvested at all," Mr. McG said. "They needed at least two more weeks in the ground." Mrs. McG and Toni moved closer to comfort him. The five of them hugged under the stars.

The next summer, Mr. McG planted his cash crop in the main garden. They had room to spare, and the plants would be safer there. Rafe favored rigging up booby traps to stop potential thieves, but Mr. McG worried about Toni and her friends. "The most important thing you and Sunny can do is not tell anyone about these plants, no matter how trustworthy you think they are. If these babies make it full term, we'll be able to get a VCR this Christmas." Rafe crossed his fingers. The whole family wanted a VCR.

When the plants reached two feet, Mr. McG put a lock on the garden gate. When they were a month from maturity, he set up a tent next to the garden. He and Toni spent the first night in what he considered his guard house. Toni thought it was fun. Rafe took the second night and thought it was fun too. Sunny volunteered for the third. She wanted the VCR more than anyone.

After a few nights, the parents realized how casually they'd placed their children in a potentially dangerous situation. A transistor radio left running inside the tent replaced live bodies. As she helped her mom make applesauce that night, Toni said, "Someone left the radio on in the tent. I turned it off when I went out to lock the henhouse."

Mrs. McG watched Toni turn the handle on the food mill and tried to think of a good explanation for why the radio should be left on. She couldn't. She said, "That's good."

They replaced the radio with a baby monitor they bought for $29.00. Mrs. McG told Toni, "With this we'll be able to hear if deer get into the garden." They placed the microphone end in the garden and plugged it into a waterproof extension cord running into the master bedroom. Mr. and Mrs. McG didn't sleep well that first night. The monitor magnified sounds. Their room sounded like a Grade B movie, *The Revenge of the Giant Crickets.*

An hour after the family left for school and work the next morning, Mrs. McG heard a suspicious sound on the monitor. She dashed out of the house and ran halfway to the garden before she realized she didn't have a plan. What would she do if someone really was there? "Unhand those plants, you villain!" She decided she'd try to scare them off from a safe distance. "Rafe! Come quick," she called even though he wasn't home. That succeeded in frightening off their orange cat who had been rolling around in dry leaves and proved equally successful on subsequent forays in frightening off families of California quail.

Everyone else laughed at these stories, but being in charge during the day and not sleeping well at night combined to leave Mrs. McG a wreck. When Toni's bunny, Peter, disappeared, Mrs. McG said it was the last straw. She broke down and cried with Toni.

Peter Rabbit lived on their deck. They hadn't wanted him to spend his life caged, but now he was missing.

"I don't understand how he got out," said Mr. McG. "He can't jump to the top of the rail, and he can't squeeze through the slats."

"I've heard you guys talking about thieves around here. Do you think someone stole Peter Rabbit, Dad?" Toni's big brown eyes filled with tears again.

"I'm sure no one would steal your bunny," said Mr. McG firmly. "We're going to find him." And they did. They heard him on the monitor. Peter Rabbit was in Mr. McGregor's garden, nibbling Swiss chard.

Mrs. McG spent most of the next day going between the deck and the garden, the garden and the deck, checking on Peter's whereabouts and suspicious noises on the monitor.

After living with the monitor twenty-four hours a day for two weeks, they recognized the sounds of birds, falling leaves, dewdrops, raindrops, rabbits, cats, breezes, and the neighbor's dog on a midnight prowl. When the night of the big noise came, they knew this was it. The intruder sounded bigger than a dog or a deer, much bigger. Mr. McG ran out into the night wearing only his Tai Chi slippers. Just outside the door, he saw a shadow of such unexpected proportions that his mind blanked for a moment. It wasn't a man. It was...a pony? No one in their neighborhood had a pony, but it was definitely a pony grazing on their lawn. The intruder wanted their grass, but not the kind they'd worried about.

They didn't turn the monitor off until Mr. McG harvested. Santa brought their VCR that Christmas, but their crops were numbered. Planes from The Campaign Against Marijuana Planting spied in the Sonoma County skies, taking pictures. CAMP discovered marijuana and busted people with as few as one or two plants. They finally showed up at the McGregors, five cars carrying eleven armed men. Toni and Jim, Sunny's sweetheart, were the only ones at the house. An officer said to Toni, "It'll go easier on your dad if you tell us where he keeps his stuff."

The little girl didn't have to decide if she would rat on her dad or not because she only knew where plants grew. CAMP already knew that much from their aerial photographs. They ripped the five plants out of the ground and took them away. There were fines, legal fees, mandatory drug rehabilitation meetings, years of probation.

A space stayed empty in their garden the following summer. "What is this?" asked Mrs. McG. "Is it a memorial grass plot?"

"You can plant something there, if you want," said Mr. McG.

"That's all right. I just wondered."

They never planted anything in that spot again. Gardening wasn't as much fun for Mr. McGregor when he couldn't play scientist, controlling the sex of his plants and whether or not they produced seeds. Each summer he planted less until one summer he planted nothing at all. Now the entire garden has gone to weed.

Goblin, a Love Story

Doris B. Murphy

My beautiful dog, Goblin, was born on Halloween, but there was nothing spooky about him. Even as a puppy, he gazed thoughtfully at people, walked sedately, and never frolicked as most puppies do. He would smile, but I never saw him laugh. His mother was a labrador and his father a collie, so that he had inherited a sturdy build along with distinctive brown and white markings.

When I took him to obedience school he behaved with decorum, glancing scornfully at the frisky young dogs who embarrassed their owners. As an adult, he assumed his duties as our protector with resolve and attention. He would circle the house twice before coming to the car to greet me. Then he would smile as if to say, *All clear. You are safe now.*

Our house on fifteen acres of open land and ancient redwood trees outside Occidental faced east where we could watch the sun rise. The early morning air was pure and sweet with the fragrance of redwoods and bay trees. Each day Goblin would walk his domain and then sit under his favorite tree. Peace and quiet ruled in our corner of the world, until Goblin fell in love. Two dogs moved into the house down the hill, a tough and unfriendly pit bull named Butch, and a pretty flirty girl-dog called Sheba. Goblin was immediately taken with Sheba and she with him.

Butch noted the attraction between Sheba and Goblin. He bared his teeth and growled. *No way. Lay off, she's mine.* When Goblin continued to court Sheba, Butch went for Goblin's jugular vein. Goblin limped back up the hill, bloody but not defeated. Butch's owners built a fence to discourage dog visiting. Goblin jumped over it; Butch dug under it. To isolate Sheba, her owners tied her to the doghouse. One day, she tried to jump the fence to join Goblin, but her leash was too short. Her owners found her strangled, hanging half on one side, half on the other side of the fence. She had died for love.

With Sheba gone, Butch and Goblin remained mortal enemies. Goblin could not accept being outmatched. His need for revenge increased with each encounter. He would sit for hours on the crest of the hill exchanging insults with Butch.

Goblin did not lose his dignity after battling Butch, but he lost some of his beauty. His lovely face became scarred. His hip, which had been badly mangled on more than one occasion, gave him pain. Sometimes he limped, but he would not allow me to comfort him or give him an aspirin. As he walked to his lookout under the fir tree, his soft brown eyes said, *I'll be okay. Just leave me be.*

On one encounter Butch fastened his jaw to Goblin's upper lip and hung there until he ripped my dog from snout to forehead. After plastic surgery by his devoted Doctor Bowles, a week in the hospital, and a huge medical bill, I hoped this might be the end of the feud. Dr. Bowles was proud of his surgical skills and told other dog-owners about his patient, the indomitable Goblin.

Goblin was now nine-years-old and Butch twelve. They rested and ignored each other during the long winter. But in the spring of that year, love bloomed again for Goblin. A glorious golden retriever named Rollie moved in down the road to the north of us, where no dog had lived before. Rollie was young and sweet-tempered. Butch wasn't interested, so there was no competition from that direction. Goblin and Rollie frolicked. I had never seen him so animated. He laughed with his eyes sparkling and his mouth wide open as he and Rollie raced from her house to his and back again. I thought his troubles were at an end, and that only happiness lay ahead.

One hot August day, Woodrow, a small male terrier who was always confined to his quarters, broke free and wandered into our front yard. Goblin was away visiting pregnant Rollie. I stood by the front gate with Woodrow, holding him by his broken leash while waiting for his owner to claim him. Just as she arrived, Goblin sauntered up the road looking pleased with himself. Then he saw the other male dog. Swiftly and without warning, he pounced on Woodrow, ripping the rope from my hands. I screamed at him to stop, but he ignored me. I pounded on his back demanding and pleading. Woodrow never had a chance. When Goblin finally let go, Woodrow's owner and I stood stunned, the small body of the terrier on the ground between us.

Goblin walked back towards Rollie's house without looking at me. He had vanquished another potential rival. Was he proud of himself? There was no spring to his step. I didn't call him back, unsure of what I felt. Angry with him? Not really. In a way I understood. Woodrow's owner picked him up, put him on the seat beside her, and drove off without speaking to me.

I didn't see Goblin for two days. He'd never spent a night away from home. On the evening of the second day, I was outside watering the roses when Goblin appeared at the front gate. He gave me a long thoughtful look but he did not come inside. He just stood there, seeming to ask, *Are you mad at me? Am I forgiven? May I come in?*

Although I was relieved to see him, I did not invite him in, nor did I greet him lovingly. I said instead, "Bad, bad dog."

He turned and walked away. I thought how sad he looked and that I would hug him when he returned. I never saw him again. I asked the neighbors if they had seen him. They had not. No one volunteered to help me look for him. It was as if there were a conspiracy of silence. Had he been killed for retribution? Or was he wandering somewhere up in the hills, homeless and ashamed? The thought that my proud and dignified dog might be starving, his coat filthy, his brown eyes dulled, sends arrows of pain to my heart.

Once around the Lake

Eileen Clegg

The minute hand on the old oak-framed wall clock signaled five o'clock. Most of the clerical staff gathered jackets and purses and began filing out the door. Maria remained sitting behind her desk with a stack of file folders nestled in her ample lap.

A young woman rushed up with her arms full of files. "Maria, I know you always stay late and I've got to boogie so I can make my aerobics class. Could you take these back for me?"

"Of course," Maria said. She reached up, took the files, and added them to her stack.

Maria waited for the shuffling exodus to end, then rose and stretched her strong, stocky body. She carried the stack back to the file room, a musty-smelling place filled with decades of paper. She returned the files to their slots, removed the cards that had marked their absence, then moved the cards into plastic containers where they waited for the next day, when more files would be taken out, shuffled through, and put back. Maria had heard people say that computers could do the work better. But this was her job, part of the program the Social Service Department had prescribed for her.

One of the managers met her as she came out of the file room. "Still here, Maria?"

"Yes."

"How was your day?" he asked.

"It was a day," she responded, knowing that she was violating her program just a bit with that answer. Part of the program was learning professionalism and professionalism meant always saying "fine" when someone asked how you were even if you were trying to calm a drunken husband until midnight and then woke up at 2:00 a.m. to comfort a screaming child.

"Good night, Maria."

She walked back to the kitchen area and looked at the stacks of cups with sticky brown rings and congealed milky coffee. She filled them with warm water and dish soap, rinsed the pot, and looked up at the sign on the wall. "Please clean up after yourself. Your mother doesn't work here." She smiled. Few people picked up after themselves. After all, a mother did work here.

Strange. The government paid people to look after her children during the day so she could work. She left her children so she could look after adults. Replacing files, replacing tinker toys, what was the difference? Except that she loved her children and didn't mind their messes.

Maria carried a damp paper towel back to clean her desk, picked up the phone, and dialed the number of her social worker, Janet.

"How goes it?" Janet's voice came over the line.

"It was a day," Maria said, smiling. She knew her social worker would understand what she meant by that.

"How are you sleeping? Any more dreams, Maria?"

"The same two. One or the other almost every night."

In one dream, Joe is dead and Maria stands frozen beside him, knowing she has unwillingly participated in his death, somehow, because he had to be put out of his misery. In the other dream, she and Joe are at a picnic table near Spring Lake, as they were as teenagers. He's kissing her and she's laughing, filled with desire for him. The kissing dream brings back the powerful rush of love. The killing dream brings relief and guilt.

"Well," Janet said. "Maybe one day you'll bring those two images together. You know how I feel. Pillow fight."

They both laughed The joke had begun three months ago when Janet asked Maria to trace the scar above her eyebrow where Joe had cut her. Janet had tried to get Maria to hit a pillow to work out her feelings toward Joe. Maria tossed the pillow back and said she didn't feel anything. Janet just stared, mystified at Maria. "I'm sorry," Maria said. She couldn't conjure up the right feeling at the right time.

Janet tossed the pillow to Maria again and said, "Quit apologizing!"

Maria glared at her, "Sorry for apologizing," and threw the pillow back. They tossed the pillow back and forth until the end of the session when Maria had said *yes* to the re-entry program designed to keep single mothers out of the welfare system.

"I'm off for my walk around the lake now," Maria told Janet. They agreed to talk again in a week and said goodbye.

Maria pulled off her black, simulated leather heels. Janet had said Maria was to have special time of her own once a week. Maria had chosen a walk around Spring Lake. The lake was 2.3 miles around and Maria now walked it in an hour.

As she pulled on her thick white socks and Reebok tennis shoes, she admired her legs, thick but strong, good legs for somebody thirty-four with three children. She stood and caught her reflection in the glass of one of the office cubicles, surprised by her round face framed by the new hairstyle her sixteen-year-old daughter had created this morning. She'd taken Maria's bangs and teased them, sprayed them, and curled her bobbed hair with a curling iron.

"I want you to look nice, Mom." Maria had heard the pride in her daughter's voice.

Slinging her tote bag over her shoulder, Maria headed down the courthouse steps to her old Volkswagen. She drove across town in ten minutes, parked, and walked quickly toward the lake. Spring Lake never changed. It was a comforting refuge with twisted oak trees and cooling shade alongside warm, open meadows. Years ago, they'd had fun in the park. Then it became her place of escape with the children. Away from the thick atmosphere in their troubled apartment, Maria used to sit by the lake and convince herself that Joe had reasons for being angry and frustrated.

He had tried so hard to succeed. He went to college and had dreams for his future. Then the children came. Jobs began, jobs ended, and Joe grew more desperate each time. Maria became his shock absorber. She understood that. When a man starts to yell or starts to hit, you somehow leave your body and become a container for that anger. Where else would the shocks go?

Then she discovered that Joe had been worse to the children than to her. She knew he was rough with them but she didn't know how rough until a neighbor called the police one day when she wasn't home. Next, the social worker came, then the restraining order, the court dates, and the program to help them live without Joe. Twice since the restraining order, Joe had burst into their new little apartment, grabbed the baby, and threatened to take him away. Maria learned *strategies* to deal with these situations and, so far, they had worked. But what if he went too far before the police got there some day? What would she do then?

Maria was nearing the end of her walk, only about a quarter-mile to her car. Thinking made the time go fast. But her breath came hard and short. She concentrated on her feet. No tiptoeing, no light walking, firm steps on the ground.

Up ahead, two people stood in her path about 100 feet away. Youths, one brown and one white. They looked to be about sixteen or seventeen. As she got closer, the white one threw her a challenging stare with a twisted smile. Maria felt an electric shock. So familiar. Warning. Danger.

Her legs kept moving automatically. She could go around the boys. Or she could go back. But wouldn't it be obvious that she was changing direction because of them? And wouldn't that let them know she was afraid? There was more danger when somebody thought you were afraid. She would keep going and they would probably leave her alone. The white boy, who was wearing a brown, cracked-leather jacket, put a hand on his hip and stared at Maria.

"Hey, I didn't know they had whales in Spring Lake," he yelled at her with a bitter laugh. Her legs kept moving, forward on her path.

"Go, Mama, make some waves." He yelled louder this time.

Was he threatening her? What did these boys want with a chubby older woman? Maria's thoughts spun in wild circles, but had no effect on her legs, which just kept moving, one in front of the other, firmly on the ground, not tiptoeing, not slowing down.

When she was about ten feet away, the white boy unzipped his pants and began to urinate in the path. It was suddenly clear; he would do anything to make her move. She could just walk around. Maria started to step off the path into the ankle-high weeds when he spoke again. "Check it out, Mama, this is how I mark territory."

Maria looked at him, looked him in his small eyes. He laughed, then the brown kid echoed with a hoarse chuckle that sounded forced. Maria's legs were carrying her right back to the path, advancing toward them. She could smell the urine. She stopped about one foot from them and the urine splashed on her Reeboks, mixed with dirt from the path. She did not speak.

The white boy buttoned his pants and clasped his buckle. Maria stood still, face-to-face with the boy, unable to move. The longer she stood, the more twisted his smile became. He was mad; it was in his face. He wanted her to move, badly. She was someone who just about always did what other people wanted. But now she could not get her legs to move.

"Get out of my way, bitch," the white boy spat.

Ducks quacked in the water. In her mind's eye was a picture of her children's faces. If something happened to her, where would they go? If she were to run now, where would she go? And how would that feel? Humiliating. The contorted angry face of the boy brought Joe to her mind. She could see Joe ready to hit. She wondered now, as she had never wondered during their fights, what if she had hit him back, just once? The silence seemed to stretch out and pull her thoughts back into her body. Her feet felt like lead, weighted to the ground.

"No," Maria said. It didn't sound like her voice. It was strong, loud, almost threatening.

One of the ducks banged its wings against the water. Other ducks joined the commotion. The boys turned to look. Maria knew again that she could run. There was no sign that they were armed, but they could be. She could not stop herself now. She wanted to stop this boy from ever looking like that again at any woman.

The brown youth touched the shoulder of his friend's leather jacket. "C'mon, man. Chill."

The white boy shuffled in an awkward, childlike movement. His face showed his youth, the nose pudgy, lacking the definition that comes with adulthood. He was stuck now with a need to prove his worth, willing to fight a woman to show he might prevail over someone, anyone. Pity weakened Maria's stance, her resolve began to leak away, and she wanted to hide her face so she wouldn't see his pain. But she continued watching his eyes.

A slight tightening of his facial muscles changed his pathetic, confused look back to a menacing glare. His hand tightened into a fist. An invisible switch went off in Maria's brain and adrenaline pulsed through her veins. She would not allow him to hurt her. From deep within her, a sound came out, a low animal wail that swelled into a thunderous, wounded cry vibrating through the trees and growing louder, becoming a shrill scream from a nightmare. "No, you. Not me. You. You move. GET AWAY FROM ME!"

The brown boy held up a hand as though to ward her off and turned to his friend. "Don't mess with her. The woman's insane, man." The white boy stepped backwards. Maria took a deep, shaky breath and felt the white hot rage rise again. Her arms began to flail and the scream came once more, this time without words, but louder than the first. She leaped high over the muddy puddle of urine. The boys started walking quickly in the opposite direction, muttering "Bitch! Shit! Crazy!"

Maria ran for a couple of minutes, then slowed down for a breath and looked over her shoulder. The boys were running, too. Away from her. She stopped and watched until they were gone. Then she turned to focus on the path ahead. Tears and sweat blurred her vision, but she knew the way. And she didn't have far to go.

Rock Salt and Nails

Michele Anna Jordan

If the young men were horses, if the young men were quails
If the young men were squirrels with them high bushy tails
I'd fill up my shotgun with rock salt and nails   —Bruce Philips

One St. Patrick's Day, back in the '70s when Sonoma County was still the country and Lakeville best described as a hamlet, a friend asked me to spend the day with him, his new girlfriend, and a friend who was going through a divorce. After brunch at a local restaurant, Dean suggested we could go back to my house for music and beer. Maybe I would cook corned beef and cabbage, he added shyly.

I recognized his friend's name, and knew better still the famous wife who had recently left him. They were both musicians who sang in a slow country style that appealed to me briefly, largely because I had fallen for a singer in a country band. He was married and there are few better introductions to country music than adultery. These were the days when hippies were discovering the honky-tonk, thanks to Graham Parsons, who had died recently, and to Emmylou Harris, who carried his torch. Country music sounded good for the first time in my life. I offered to make dinner.

The day was pleasant from the start. Dean's new girlfriend Molly and I dressed for the day in colorful green dresses that brushed the ground when we walked. I wore a flower in my hair in honor of my ancestors. Though I knew few of my Irish relatives, I had seen photographs and recognized the freckles, the red hair, the skin that hates the sun. While I prepared dinner, the others sat in the living room picking their guitars and singing, or, in Molly's case, sitting and occasionally joining in.

The guys drank Bushmills and Guinness throughout the day, but I didn't pay much attention. I felt remarkably free, after several months of nursing my own romantic bruises.

I wondered if Dean was attempting a little cupid action between his friend and me, but nothing except Gil's presence suggested it. There was no energy between us, and no attempts on Dean's or Molly's parts to throw us closer together, no subtle seating arrangements, no suggestion that Gil help me with dinner. I was not attracted to him, but I could see from his eyes that he was suffering. I felt compassionate and so was accommodating.

As they sang into the night, I made a request. "Rock Salt and Nails," I said, and they slipped quickly into a haunting version of one of the best revenge songs ever written by a wronged lover. They gave the song a mournful quality—using the original words of "ladies" instead of "young men," as I had first heard it sung by Gil's ex-wife—evoking the emotional landscape beneath the vengeful desire. I was glad I had not been drinking. I was not immune to the emotions the song calls forth, and I prefer not to cry in front of strangers. A little revenge, or the spirit thereof, might have revived me, but they sang without bitterness and with a resignation I struggled against daily.

For once, I felt calm and satisfied, if a little wistful, the most recent broken heart well on the mend, the next a couple of years in the future. I was a generous hostess, letting the mournful singing and picking go on much longer than was interesting, accommodating their self-indulgence with a sort of distracted expansiveness, a generosity born of the fact that I wanted nothing from either of these two guys. At some point late in the evening, Dean and Gil both lapsed into a silly Irish brogue, and I went along as best I could, awkwardly trying to put the turns and twists into my voice and to follow the strange syntax they were conjuring out of their blurred Bushmills exuberance. As they packed up and headed out the door, we continued our banter. Dean and Molly drove off first, and as I said good-bye to Gil, I offered a bit of country hospitality, thinking I could master a southern drawl more easily than a brogue. I called him *pahdner* and said something about a horse and a watering hole. I attempted a few more drawling exchanges, but I was in over my head with this country stuff and I knew it. I closed the door.

I waited until he drove away, turned off the porch light, and went to my room, leaving the front door unlocked as I always did in those days. I slipped out of my dress, into a long golden nightgown, and between the covers of my bed, a bed that I had slept in since birth, and that had been my father's before it had been mine. It was coarse-finished walnut, large and dark, with a carved headboard and footboard. I liked the bed, with its ancient sagging mattress and blue velvet quilt, which I pulled up under my chin against the cool Lakeville night, and I turned toward the window, curled up and cozy. It had been a good day.

I was on the precipice of sleep when I felt a presence, thinking at first that I was in that heightened state between waking and sleeping when strange creatures manifest themselves in the eerie light of dreams. I had cried out more than once over the years only to have the bedside image fade as the sound of my own voice fully awakened me. But no, this image had substance. Startled, I turned over and could barely make out a figure standing next to the bed.

Paralyzed by near sleep, I tried to speak but before I could form words, the figure spoke, "Well, Ah decided to take you up on your kind offer, ma'am." Adrenaline jump-started all of my faculties and I could see standing before me in the near black of Lakeville in the small hours of morning, the drunken musician, completely naked. Lord have mercy, I thought, how do I get out of this one gracefully?

Many things raced through my head in those first seconds of hesitation. I guess some women would have just brought the guy back to reality quickly and harshly, but I felt nearly as protective of him as I did of myself. Perhaps it is because I have such a mortal terror of public humiliation that I try to protect others from the same kind of exposure. For some reason, I felt no sense of physical danger. This was not an imminent rape. And so I took his hand ever so gently, as one would take the hand of a frightened child, and told him to sit down. As he did, his naked leg brushed against my arm.

"I think there's been a misunderstanding, and I apologize if I gave you the wrong impression," I said softly. I was glad it was dark, that it was a moonless night, because I'm sure he blushed from head to toe.

"I was just letting you know that you could feel like a friend and stop by if you found yourself in Lakeville. Perhaps I said things I didn't understand. But you had better go."

"Oh, God…I'm…I'm sorry," he muttered as he rose from the bed and stumbled out of my room. I heard him dressing quickly and awkwardly. He left with considerably more sound effects than he had arrived.

He called the next morning and apologized for being "a drunk old fool," as he put it. I thanked him and told him not to worry. Our paths didn't converge again for years, but lately I've come across him playing music. We have been introduced a couple of times and although there has never been a flicker of recognition in his eyes, I always smile politely, meet his gaze, and, taking my revenge where I find it, remind him that we've met.

Traveling Appetites

Marianne Ware

Harriet and Les live in a house under the redwoods of western Sonoma County. Though every growing thing around them is now at its lushest, Harriet is bored by the scenery. After an intense year of teaching, she wants to drive to Vancouver. Les, a recently retired furniture maker, hates traveling. He can't forget the '30s when his Dust Bowl refugee family drove from Texas to California in a rickety Essex, suffering from heat, hunger, and homesickness. Luckily Harriet has perfected argumentation and persuasion, along with guilt-tripping: "You swore; you gave your word; you said we'd definitely go." As a result, Les is actually making preparations, albeit grudgingly.

"I'll have to bring everything. Not likely we'll find our kind of food in Canada." After decades of indiscriminate eating, Les is now a devotee of the McDougall Diet. He's adamant that they stay on this total vegetarian, no-dairy-or-added-oil regimen because of Harriet's diabetes and joint problems, plus his family's history of heart and kidney trouble.

Les reads his "Must Bring" list to Harriet:

> brown rice
> textured vegetable protein
> unsalted, no fat pretzels
> McDougall soups and pasta cups
> rice crackers
> low sodium canned garbanzo beans
> vegetarian pintos

"Better pack the GasEx," she tells him. "We'll be in awfully close quarters."

Les continues for two more pages. "No one'll believe we stuck to our diet the whole damned vacation. Maybe you can write a piece for a travel magazine and call it, 'Vegans on the Highway.'" This presumption annoys her. Harriet has stories of her own to finish, once she gets over her dry spell.

She sighs and goes to look for their suitcases. Packing is her jurisdiction, as is postcard-writing from the motel rooms she secures for them. But what if the beds are saggy, and she can't keep her promise to have frequent, unrestrained sex with him? Vacations are supposedly a time when even long-married folk rekindle their passions. Harriet certainly needs rekindling, though Les is still the handsomest man in the world to her with the best-looking rear south of the Siskiyous. She daydreams about making love to him, but is usually tense and tired at bedtime. She claims it's her arthritis.

Despite their marriage's difficulties, Harriet loves Les and adores their division of labor. For a year now, he has done all the cooking, and though the diet is austere, it's helped her blood sugar and high cholesterol while melting over half of her excess pounds away. Les' controlling is good for me, she frequently reminds herself.

"I'm going to fix every meal in the rice cooker," Les calls to her. "We'll need to take non-fat tortillas and steel-cut oats with the rest of the stuff."

On Friday morning, June 15, they're off and driving. Five minutes from home, Harriet opens a box of Snyder's pretzels, the salted kind she'd "accidentally" dropped into their shopping cart. Soon Les complains: "Should have exchanged these…too much sodium…thirsty." It's Harriet's job to jerk the water jug up from the floor of the back seat and fill their glasses. She winces because the jug is wedged and she has a stiff shoulder.

It will take several hours before they get to the Arcata Motor Lodge with the indoor pool she once enjoyed so much. Harriet has forgotten if this is the place with double beds only. Picturing six-foot Les with his feet dangling makes her anxious.

Now it's l0:30 a.m. They've been on the road for barely an hour, but Harriet's bladder speaks to her. As usual, Les complains about stopping. "It's because I've had three kids, your kids," Harriet reminds him.

"Thirty years ago," he counters.

After a pit stop at Burger King in Ukiah, she is relieved when they drive away without Les suggesting they eat their packed-at-home lunch on one of the establishment's outdoor tables, using its utensils, mustard packets, and napkins.

As they head for the freeway, Les launches into one of his doomsday health bulletins, "Burger joints are poisoning America. Soon, everyone'll be lining up for by-pass surgery, but only McDougall can save them."

Harriet punches the radio on. As if on cue, KSRO's announcer says, "Stay tuned at 1:00 p.m. for Dr. McDougall's question and answer program." Les grins with anticipation.

Approaching Willits at about noon, Harriet feels the bathroom urge again. "Look, look, there's a rest stop; let's eat lunch here."

A few minutes later, they are companionably munching Les' homemade vegeburgers on Alvarado Street buns with bean sprouts, red onion, and tomato slices.

"Just think, if the whole world ate like this…" Les, who hates it if Harriet talks when she eats, is talking and eating.

Her mind cannot bear to imagine it, the collapse of the meat, dairy, fish, and chicken industries, no one selling Velveeta, pork ribs, milkshakes, or Mounds candy bars. At least someone should be able to enjoy them.

Now she is thinking of the friends they plan to visit in Grants Pass, ample Alice and 300-pound Dwayne.

"We need to get A and D on the diet," Les pronounces.

Even though she's used to his mind reading, Harriet is startled. "You promised no proselytizing!"

Silence.

After a walk several times around the parking lot, and another trip to the bathroom for Harriet, they get back into the car just in time for the manic theme music of *The Doctor McDougall Show.*

Les' guru begins with a report on milk as the cause of child-hood leukemia. Harriet has heard it all before at a McDougall seminar. Now she's thinking of the ghastly aorta of a dead cholesterol junky McDougall displayed for the audience, plus the two glass stomachs. One contained a dab of gooey fat and the other was filled to the rim with corn kernels. "Both provide the same calories, but which one is going to fill you up and keep you healthy?" McDougall asked the assembled.

"COOORN!" sang the enraptured audience.

"Time for telephone calls," McD. is now saying. Harriet likes this part of the show better than his lecturing which reminds her of certain full-of-themselves English Department colleagues.

Les snorts when the first caller asks, "But if I don't eat meat, how do I get my protein?" The second voice is hostile. "It's your fault my wife don't cook good no more!" The next is an obvious convert, trying to impress the doctor. "I'm totally on the diet, one hundred percentile." McD. promptly traps him into admitting he feasts once-a-month on braised tofu. "If you really mean to get healthy cut the soy products!" the doctor chides him. Then a timorous woman calls to say, "I'm on the diet, but worried about my, uh, change in elimination…"

"How often do you go?"

"Several times a…"

"Perfect! Three or four unformed stools a day is absolutely normal."

"Unformed? Normal?"

Harriet can't suppress a chuckle.

"You know he's right." Les insists. "Look how much better we are."

"Yes, I know it! I know it."

Some time later, Harriet realizes she's slept through the rest of the program, that the station is out of range now, and that they're way past Garberville. "Aren't we near that Paul Bunyan and Babe-the-Blue-Ox place?" She smiles, remembering those huge plaster statues, come-ons for a touristy gift shop and restaurant. Once she made Les take her picture standing under Babe's belly, her hand on his gigantic robin's-egg-colored scrotum.

"No, that's way past Arcata. Look at the map and figure how far the motel is." Les wants Harriet to return to her duties.

"It's still a couple of hours." She feels the familiar pressure down under. "Look for a rest stop."

"This is your fifth time."

"It is not!" Harriet is indignant. If he keeps challenging her body's needs, the vacation will be ruined. It's different back in

Sonoma County. She knows the location of every public rest-room, from the stenchy, graffitied one in Cotati's town square, to that spotless cubbyhole behind Cloverdale's Foster Freeze.

Suddenly Les pulls off 101 and into a service station. There, both he and Harriet scurry to their respective restrooms.

An hour-and-a-half later they're in Eureka where the freeway empties onto restaurant row. "Hey, remember that great Samoa Cookhouse?" Harriet is overwhelmed by nostalgia.

"The worst! The worst!" He blasts her exuberance.

"Wonderful!" She defies him. "Mounds of fried chicken, pot-roast, biscuits, gravy and yummy peach cobbler with vanilla ice…"

"Poison! How can you even think of it?"

Harriet rattles the map. "Look, our motel isn't much north of town, maybe fifteen more minutes. Can't wait to swim after all this sitting." Harriet loves the water, the only place she can move without discomfort. They do laps everyday at the Santa Rosa YMCA, companionably swimming for over an hour, both on the same silent underwater wavelength.

By the time Harriet and Les arrive at their motel, unload the suitcases, hanging clothes, several huge boxes full of non-perishable food, three ice chests, and the rice cooker, Harriet is exhausted.

"Let's take a nap, then go out to eat."

"But where?" Les looks dubious.

"Surely there's a health food restaurant."

"Not up to Vegan standards. Most vegetarian places use oil and milk products."

"Not every single one, everywhere, just that place in Bodega where you caught the chef frying."

Harriet is now in her half-slip, which she's pulled up over her bare breasts and torso. She plops down on the double, then turns sideways. It's clear Les hasn't yet noticed the bed's size, but he can't miss Harriet's Rubenesque cheeks peeking out at him. In a moment, he's next to her, breathing into her hair, the back of her neck. Now he's licking her earlobe.

"Later, after we swim," she tells him, even though some-thing is definitely stirring inside her.

Les sighs and rolls over. Now she hugs up to his back,

stroking his arm and shoulder. "I want you, honest. I'm just so stiff and sleepy."

"Yeah, yeah, later."

Harriet is surprised at how quickly Les begins snoozing. She lies awake for quite a while longer.

"Hey, get up and help me." Les' voice jerks Harriet back to consciousness as a plastic bag lands on the bed beside her. "Go wash this stuff for the salad."

In the cramped bathroom, she first relieves herself, then quickly rinses the romaine, tomato, carrot, red pepper, mushrooms, and green onions, plopping them into a handtowel.

Harriet wants to go swimming right that second.

"Not on your life," Les booms. "It's already seven o'clock. Fix the salad."

"What can we serve it in?"

"Use this," he says, handing her the ice bucket. "You can put in your story how we improvised so everything worked out perfectly."

"I suppose you brought the mustard-honey no-oil dressing?"

"In the green icebox." Les' tone tells her the salad is wholly her responsibility. But that's not fair according to their arrangement. She's only supposed to do dishes.

"Come and get it," Les announces This strikes Harriet as ridiculous, since there's no way to stride forward robustly in their motel room. All she can do is lean over the bed to grab the plate of brown rice and steamed veggies Les has heaped for her.

"Isn't this great?" he asks.

Harriet stares at him.

"I didn't think we needed salt after those pretzels."

Harriet is chewing chipmunk-style, using her front teeth only.

"Do we have pepper?"

"Who needs it?"

At last the meal is over. Only a small mound of broccoli stems and blackened mushroom bits remains on Harriet's plate. She hasn't asked for seconds.

"Hey, I almost forgot." She pulls a huge package of apricot bars from her swim bag. "I got these at Trader Joe's. It's okay for our kind of diet." She opens it, selects two bars, and begins munching both simultaneously, ignoring their strong sulfur smell and stale texture.

"Here, let me see that." Les grabs the package and begins reading: "Pureed Apricots, Well Water, Lemon Juice, Flour, Baking Soda and *Whey* Solids." Harriet's neck prickles.

"You know we can't eat these; whey means milk products." Les glares at her. She swallows the last bite as he dumps the rest into the trash can. "You were about to go on insulin, and I nearly had a heart attack, before McDougall." He seems to be speaking to an auditorium, though Harriet is his only audience.

"Time to exercise," she says, leaping up to grab her swimsuit, then head for the bathroom.

The pool is much too warm and crowded. "Let's get out and do our laps early in the morning," Les tells her.

Last time they had the place to themselves and swam in continuous ovals. Later she did calisthenics, then chased after Les underwater, wrapping her arms and legs around his torso and nibbling his shoulder every time she caught him.

Harriet needs the delicious feeling of weightless grace that only water affords her. "You go; I've *got* to swim," she tells Les who gives her a wounded look before dripping his way back to their motel room.

Harriet does aerobic exercises until the other guests disappear. Then she is free to glide about the entire pool as if she owned it. If only she could swim nude, if only Les were with her. She pictures his magnificent back and broad shoulders, his glorious rump, suitless. Oh oh, here comes the manager, telling her he's got to close the pool now.

The room is unlocked when she returns to it. Les seems to be sleeping. It's so dark she has to feel her way to the bathroom. With the door closed and the light on, she sees Les' trunks plopped down next to the toilet. The sink is piled high with undone dishes. "Tomorrow, tomorrow," she whispers.

Her bare body feels sleek as she moves in velvety darkness towards her husband. Quickly she slips in beside him, between sheets that seem almost silky.

Les jerks awake as her cool limbs encircle him. "Nnnnnnn," he grumbles. "Tomorrow, tomorrow."

The Congregation

Glory Leifried

The Petaluma Congregational Church, shaded by two large oak trees, sat next to Highway 101. It had been built in the middle 1800s when the highway was a dirt road between the two rural towns of Santa Rosa and Petaluma. By the 1970s, Santa Rosa had developed into a busy city with shopping malls, business centers, schools, auto dealerships, restaurants, and banks. To the south, Petaluma had remained a rural town of dairies, farms, ranches, and a few small local businesses and industries.

This morning, although the oak trees shielded the small church from the direct rays of the hot sun, the heat still penetrated the interior. Inside, large ceiling fans hummed softly, but the members of the congregation cooled themselves with hand-crafted fans.

As always at this hour on a Sunday morning, Reverend Cyrus Halloway stood at the pulpit at the front of the church and began his sermon. Reverend Halloway had been the pastor for the past twenty-five years. Today's text was "The Cause of Social and Moral Decay in America," one of Reverend Halloway's favorite sermons, one he preached over and over again. Halloway was a small man who always wore a black suit and hat, even on the hottest of days. He had small, sharp eyes and wore his glasses at the end of his nose. His tight thin lips made him appear mean. He looked like he had been the same age forever.

As Reverend Halloway looked out over the congregation, the word *sin* slowly rose from his throat. He savored the taste of it in his mouth and was about to spew it out, when he was forced to swallow it in one big gulp, almost choking. An Afro-American man, woman, and three young children had appeared at the back of the Petaluma Congregational Church.

The man ushered his family quickly into an empty pew. He nodded politely to the shocked faces while his family settled themselves. No face showed more shock than Reverend Halloway's. He cleared his throat two or three times in the direction of Deacon Lindsey Edwards, who was sitting asleep with his head bowed over his Bible.

The pastor had personally bestowed the title of deacon upon Lindsey. Born and raised in Petaluma, Lindsey had gone away to attend Gammon Theological Seminary, in Atlanta, graduated and returned home where he requested the position of Assistant Pastor of Petaluma Congregational Church. Reverend Halloway told him that a church needed only one leader; although he appreciated Lindsey's interest in the ministry. There were many duties in the service of the Lord. For ten years Lindsey had faithfully offered himself for service. On Saturday nights he made certain the church was spotless and everything ready for Sunday morning service. He was up by 6:00 a.m. to drive Reverend Halloway the twenty miles to the Denny's Restaurant in Santa Rosa for an early breakfast every Sunday. Even though Santa Rosa was numbered with the "sin cities" in his list of Sodoms and Gomorrahs, eating breakfast at Denny's was a weekly ritual for Reverend Halloway.

Most of Lindsey's duties only served Reverend Halloway and had no connection with the church. The Reverend had never offered his assistant the opportunity to conduct a Sunday service. Lindsey accepted his duties humbly and without complaint. His wife, Cynthia, did not have the same self-sacrificing spirit as her husband and complained loud and clear to him and the congregation.

The nudge of his wife's elbow against his arm sent Lindsey to his feet. His Bible fell beneath the pew in front of him. As he spoke, Reverend Halloway's small eyes bored into Lindsey.

"Brother Edwards, I see we have some visitors at the back of the church. Could you please assist them? I believe they're lost."

Lindsey looked back and recognized Charlie Porter and his family. Charlie had a small poultry and egg farm down the road from him. They had been neighbors for four years. Their children went to the same elementary school, where Charlie's wife was one of the cooks.

"I don't believe they're lost, Pastor, that's Charlie Porter and his family."

"I know who it is, Edwards. But they must be lost if they came in here. Go back there and see what they need."

"But they've already sat down."

"See to it then, man. Get a move on."

As she sat beside him, Lindsey's wife could barely control herself. "Let him do his own dirty work, Lin. I swear that old man makes me mad. All he ever does is use you."

Lindsey did not want to go back and ask Charlie why he was there. All the Porter family were obviously dressed for church. Cynthia hadn't stopped talking, "It's half your fault the way he treats you anyway. You never speak up for yourself."

As he walked to the back of the church, Lindsey felt awkward. He had talked with Charlie about a lot of different things—baseball, boxing, politics, but never about God or religion. Charlie extended his hand to Lindsey; they shook briefly.

"How are you and your family doing today, Charlie?"

"Fine, Lindsey. How are you all doing?"

"We're all doing all right, I guess." Lindsey was embarrassed to ask the next question. "Is there anything we can help your family with today, Charlie?"

"No. Everything's all right. We were invited to service today, so we came."

"Oh. I see. Well, I hope you enjoy the service. Hello there, Evelyn, how are you?

"Fine, Lindsey. How are you?"

Reverend Halloway stretched almost prostrate across his pulpit trying to glean bits of the conversation at the back of the church. He did not like the look on Lindsey's face and the Porters had not moved.

Lindsey spoke before he reached the pulpit. "No. They're not lost, Pastor. According to Charlie they were invited to attend Sunday service."

"Invited! Invited by whom? A member of this congregation?"

"It would appear so. I believe so. I mean it's only logical that…"

"I can't believe that any member of my congregation would invite those people here. In the history of this church, we have never had a Negro sit in the assembly. Did he say the word invited, Edwards?"

The Reverend's eyes panned the pews as he watched for any sign of betrayal from the congregation. Before his eyes met Roxanne Garrett's, he knew she was the one. She sat in the pew next to her husband, Matt, her small daughter on her lap. He did not see betrayal in her eyes. He saw defiance.

Reverend Halloway had always been uncomfortable around Roxanne. Since her teens, he'd suspected that she possessed a rebellious spirit and a personality he could describe as stubborn and self-willed. As a grown woman, she had not changed at all.

Roxanne had started the controversy about his rule forbidding women from wearing pants to church. Reverend Halloway remembered how she convinced all the women and nearly every man that everyone had the right to dress as they pleased. Two summers ago he had seen her leave the Community Swim Center in a bathing suit when she was eight months pregnant. Clearing his throat, Lindsey brought Halloway back to the present. "Invited."

"What?"

"He said invited."

"Well, they are going to have to be uninvited, Edwards."

"What do you mean?"

"Tell them they have to leave!"

Lindsey barely whispered, "I'm not going back there and tell Charlie and his family they have to leave. I can't."

"No reason why you can't."

"There's plenty of reasons why I can't. It's not right, for one thing."

"Right. Those people have no rights. Walking in here as bold as daylight and sitting down."

The congregation had begun to murmur.

"Edwards, in your job as assistant pastor..."

"Assistant pastor?"

"I've always looked to you for assistance, Edwards, and now I need you..."

"But you've always said that a…"

Roxanne Garrett stood up. "Although I'm sure most of you here know the Porters, I would like to introduce them as my guests today. I'm glad they accepted my invitation, and I hope they enjoy the service." She sat down.

A few people nodded their heads towards Roxanne and the Porters, but most eyes were fixed on the Reverend Halloway.

"Roxanne Garrett, you have severely overstepped your bounds this time. By whose and what authority have you invited these people here and caused disruption in my church?"

"Your church?"

"Yes."

"Since when is this your church? And the only interruption I see is you. The Porters were interested in a place of worship and I invited them here to join us."

"If you felt the need to direct these people to a place to worship, there is a fine Negro church up in Santa Rosa."

"They don't live in Santa Rosa; they live here."

"But they cannot attend church here."

"Why not?"

"They just cannot and that is all there is to it."

"That's not an answer. Why not?"

"Because they're Negroes, woman. Are you blind?"

The rest of the congregation seemed to enjoy the Reverend's displeasure.

They had not seen him this excited and on fire in years. Some had never seen him on fire. A few members rallied behind Roxanne and voiced their disapproval of the Reverend's attitude. Lindsey dared not look at Cynthia because he recognized her voice among the protesters' chorus.

Jess Tyler, one of the oldest members of the church, said, "It makes no difference to me either way, but I hope this discussion doesn't cause service to run past quitting time because I'm hungry and want to get home to dinner." He turned to the man who sat next to him and said, "I know old Halloway. You give him an inch and he'll take a mile. I like a preacher who knows how to start and finish on time."

Charlie Porter picked up one of his children, grabbed another by the hand, and stood up to leave. But his wife shook her head and refused to follow him. He sat down again. From across the room, Roxanne flashed a big smile at Mrs. Porter.

Jess Tyler rose again and spoke directly to the pastor. "Halloway, I say let the congregation vote on it and we can settle the whole thing right now."

Halloway pointed at Jess Tyler. "This is not a business meeting, Jess!"

"It might as well be; we've heard your opinion of the thing. I say vote on it."

"There's members who aren't here to have their say about it," Halloway answered.

"Then they don't have anything to say about it." Jess pointed to Lindsey and said, "Lindsey, you keep count. Now, all those in agreement to Charlie and his family joining us here, put up your hands."

Lindsey started to count the raised hands, then stopped. "Almost every hand in here is up, Jess."

"Keep counting."

"Eighty-two raised, not counting children."

Jess said, "Can't be too many left, I guess, but we'll give everybody a chance to have a say. Now, all those opposed to them joining, put up your hands."

Lindsey saw a few hands rise and drop quickly. He almost spoke, then remembered the pastor standing behind him. He turned and saw Reverend Halloway lower his arm.

Jess spoke, "That settles it, Halloway. The congregation voted on it and the Porters are welcome to join us here. Now you can get on with the service."

Reverend Halloway spoke weakly, "I'll turn the remainder of the service over to our assistant pastor, Lindsey Edwards."

Lindsey climbed the steps to the platform, and stood nervously behind the pulpit. "As Assistant Pastor of the Petaluma Congregational Church, I would like to extend the warmest welcome to our new members, the Porter family. This morning's sermon is one that has always been very close to my heart, so to speak. I've kept it folded here in my pocket for the past ten years."

Walking the Tracks to Graton

Marilyn B. Kinghorn

I have walked the tracks to Graton,

from Occidental Road through untended fields, watching the swooping flight of barn swallows. Pregnant and heavy, I balanced lightly on one rail, eating ripe, sun-warmed blackberries that stained my lips.

I have walked the tracks to Graton,

an outlaw town of three bars, three service stations, and a row of rundown buildings all watched over by a leaking water tower. I have danced at fairs in streets where the night before fights errupted, knives flashed, and shots rang out.

I have walked the tracks to Graton,

past canneries where the sweet smell of freshly picked apples gave way to the sourness of fermenting waste. The fire station's familiar siren signaled midday, releasing tired women in stained aprons, cigarettes lit as they gathered to gossip and eat cold tortillas on the loading docks.

In the center of town the dirty windows of three boarded-up storefronts reflected images of past shopkeepers and customers. Cobwebs and rat trails pockmarked the dusty shelves.

I saw Baker's Cafe and Myrtle Baker pumping gas, the smell of hot grease from her grill coming through the screened doorway.

I heard the voices of farmers and truck drivers sitting on back-less stools at her worn formica counter.

Up the street past Skip's Bar, at Turner's Garage, Selwyn Turner bent over a truck engine, only his back and legs visible. His wife, Barbara, leaned against a Volkswagon, chatting as she filled the gas tank.

I have walked the tracks to Graton,

where migrant workers gathered in front of the Bola Negra Bar, their hands wrapped around steaming paper cups, waiting for the sun and a pickup to take them to the fields or orchards.

I have walked the tracks to Graton,

discovering the strange beauty of snake lilies growing along the rails, their mottled, fleshy stalks swaying under heavy burgundy flowers that seduce flies with their dead horse smell.

I have walked the tracks to Graton,

through winter rains, spring blossoms, the golden grass of summer, and into apple harvest. Now the tracks are gone, the rails torn out. The path is overgrown with weeds and blackberry vines, fences and posted signs.

Native
Marylu Downing

We meet for the first time. I'm trying to make a good impression, but I think they're disappointed I don't fit the California image. I'm not thin, young, or blonde. In sandals I'm six feet tall, slightly taller than Jake's dad, Robert. I tower over his mother, Marion. The humidity makes my graying red hair unmanageable. Frizzy pieces spring out in all directions. I tuck a stray curl behind my ear and wish Jake's seven-year-old daughter could have come with us to ease the tension. But her mother refused permission to let her leave the state, so we're here on our own with no darling child as a distraction.

"You're from California. Live out there with all the fruits and nuts, huh?" My father-in-law laughs as he extends his right hand.

I shake hands firmly, the way my dad taught me, but I'm not sure it's the right thing here. My reflection in the glass of the front door smiles back at me, all sunshine and teeth. I'm afraid to look closely for fear I'll want to run after the cab and beg a ride back to the airport.

Their home is large, three stories high, and its elegance surprises me. Jake hasn't told me his parents are rich. I follow Marion, Robert, and Jake down the hall. The formal living room holds chintz-covered chairs and carefully arranged collections of crystal that look expensive. Robert picks up a glass dolphin, "This came from your state, my dear."

"Gumps," says Marion. She takes the dolphin from her husband and returns it gently to its place on the table.

"Jake, why don't you take Flora upstairs so she can relax before the guests arrive?" Robert asks. "Would you like martinis?"

"No martinis for us, Dad, thanks. We'll take iced tea."

"It's too bad your plane was late; doesn't give you much time to get ready," says Marion. "Flora, we're so pleased to have you here. Our friends are dying to meet you." Something about the way she says this makes me feel like a specimen. Nothing about her frosted hair or the tailored pale pink suit which perfectly fits her tiny figure reassures me.

Upstairs, Jake changes into linen pants and a white dress-shirt. He looks handsome. I wonder if his friends will think he's wasting himself on me. To calm myself I sit for a minute in my underpants to meditate. I close my eyes and wait for the "inner smile" to fill me from head to toe. It only moves about as far as my thighs. I give up and put on my rayon print dress.

"Jake, how do I look?"

"You look great," he says, pulling his blonde hair into a ponytail.

"Are you just trying to humor me?"

"Come here, Flo. Don't worry about what people might think of you. Our guests won't be able to help themselves from falling under your spell. Look what happened to me." We hug. The air is as wet as it is hot. I'm sweaty and nervous.

Jake greets old friends outside a huge tent erected on the back lawn. The party has begun, a reception to celebrate our recent marriage. More than 100 people I've never met are eager to take a look at me. I breeze along in my gauzy rayon dress which billows out like a spinnaker. The other women wear structured dresses, silk and linen pantsuits.

"I love that dress, it's so youthful and looks comfortable enough to sleep in," says Marion. Taking a deep breath, I imagine the protective suit I've constructed with my hypnotherapist before leaving on this trip. Carefully woven seapalm, poppies, redwood bark, and artichoke leaves cling to me like a second skin.

I blink and ask Marion if I can help with anything in the kitchen. A faint look of disapproval crosses her face. "Oh no, dear, the caterer will take care of everything." I'm fifteen years older than her son, and from California. Marion is probably wondering what her son sees in me. I comfort myself with the hope that she's happier with me than with Jake's former wife who left him for a lesbian lover.

Jake introduces me to family members, neighbors and friends. They all want to know what I do, where we live, and what it's like.

"I'm a journalist for a small northern California paper. Our town is tiny, coastal, a fishing village really," I say. I want them to know how special our home is, want them to picture it, the boats, whales, and pelicans, but I can't. My jaws ache from constant smiling, from trying not to say the wrong thing.

I might be the curiosity, but Jake holds everyone's attention with his stories about California.

"No MacDonald's in our town. It's fish tacos or nutburgers."

"Well, I can understand the nutburgers!" Everyone laughs.

"Hey, there's this guy in our county who makes a fortune creating sacred drumming sites for his clients. I've got another friend who sells his gourmet lettuce for $8.99 a pound."

"What? Does anybody buy it?"

"It's usually sold out!"

Jake continues: "Once I saw a sign at the border, 'Leaving California, Resume Normal Behavior.'"

"That's great!" His friends are loving this.

He leaves out the festivals for banana slugs, garlic, and poison oak and the aura repair booths at the Health and Harmony Faire that we go to every spring.

I laugh with everybody else but feel like shouting, "What about eagles, the coast, the tallest trees in the world?" I'm hot and irritated and would give almost anything right now for a cool blackberry smoothie.

Upstairs in the guest room after the reception, I confront Jake.

"Turncoat! Why did you make those jokes about our home? Transplants like you have ruined California. There's too many of you; you use up our state and then you make fun of us." I take off my dress.

"Come on, Flo, you're overreacting. I love California. I consider myself a Californian!" Jake unbuttons his shirt.

"I'm fourth-generation. You followed some guru to my home state twelve years ago." I unbuckle my sandals.

"I learned a lot from Father Baba, and don't forget your ancestors stole the state from the Mexicans and Indians." Jay unzips his pants and takes them off.

"Some of my ancestors *were* the Mexicans. Anyway, I don't think your friends like me." I dig my T-shirt out of the suitcase and pull it on.

"Maybe *you* just don't like *them!*" He bangs shut the lid of the hamper.

"Your friends all have little babies and I'm practically a grandmother."

"I don't give a damn about your age. I love you, and my family and friends will grow to love you. Things don't happen immediately here. This isn't California."

"That's for damn sure!"

"You need to lighten up, Flo." Jake ambushes me with a flying tackle onto the antique bed which creaks alarmingly. We make love on the floor, afraid that the bed might collapse and we'd fall through to the first floor crushing important vases, old pictures, and glass animals. Afterward, we hold hands in the bed and fall into an exhausted sleep.

I dream of life-sized glass animals, dolphins, seals, and mountain lions pouring out from tourist shops onto the Coast Highway. They clatter and clank as they walk, casting rainbow colors on the trees. I hear the screeching of brakes and the sound of glass breaking. My heart is pounding when I wake up. It's pouring rain, and thunder rattles the empty metal hangers in the closet. If we were in California, we'd think earthquake. I get my dream journal from the suitcase and record the details of the dream, mulling over the meaning, the fragile beauty of the animals.

We've been here a week. Jake has eaten his way through his hometown, overcooked vegetables, steaks, creamed potatoes, scalloped potatoes, shiny red Jell-O salad, and biscuits with thick gravy for breakfast. Comfort food is supposed to remind us of how we grew up. I grew up eating walnut sandwiches, yogurt, chicken mole and quesadillas. There was never a biscuit with gravy on it.

Tonight we're having a last family dinner at Aunt Sylvie's.

"These are for you, Flora; I understand you're a vegetarian. Tofu balls," she explains.

"Thanks, how thoughtful of you." She also serves sweet corn on the cob and delicious artichokes with aioli.

"Blueberry Crisp, Aunt Sylvie's specialty!" Jake's sister Sarah sits down next to me and hands me a piece of crisp mounded with whipped cream. The cream isn't on my McDougall diet, so I scoop it off and eat the crisp. Crisp isn't on the diet either, but I just can't resist. I tell myself it's mostly fruit.

"What was Jake like when he was little?" I ask Sarah.

"He loved plants even then and had a huge vegetable garden. The neighbors bought lettuce, radishes, and rutabaga from him. Antonio, our gardener, taught him a lot. They really loved spending hours together discussing plants and digging in the garden. When Jake went off to college to study botany, both he and Antonio cried. Jake's always been a kind of a lovable nutcase, rescuing birds, collecting weird seed pods, things like that. And cracking us up at the dinner table. I love him a lot."

"Me too," I add between bites of crisp.

Our week here ends. We quietly box wedding gifts for shipping and pack our suitcases. "Jake, I feel that I know these people a little bit, and they know me. I think we like each other."

"I'm glad. It was great to see my old buddies, my family, but I'm looking forward to being back home," Jake says, touching my cheek.

"Don't ever expect me to move here!" I say.

"No chance of it. Why do you think I moved?" We kiss.

The cab driver honks. We hurry down two flights of stairs to say goodbye to Robert and Marion on the front steps.

"Flora, my son is lucky to have you for his wife. Now, watch out for earthquakes!"

I don't mention the San Andreas Fault which runs out to sea just one town up the coast from our home. "Thanks for everything. Come out and visit us," I say.

"I was out there a lot after the war, but California's not for me. The pace is too fast and I'm too old," says Robert.

"I know what you mean; sometimes I feel the same way." The words slip out despite my resolve to avoid any references to my age.

"Oh nonsense, you're a native, and I like that. It's great to have a daughter-in-law who is so candid and charming."

For a moment I don't know what to say. My guard is down, my protective suit forgotten.

"Robert, I hope we'll be able to spend time together when it's not so hectic."

"We'll make a point of it, Flora."

"Call me Flo, that's what I'm called back home."

"We would drive you to the airport but I have a golf tournament and Marion's got an appointment with her doctor."

Robert is about to say something more when Marion points to her watch. "We don't want you to miss your plane. Give our darling granddaughter a kiss and tell her we expect her for part of next summer. And we're dying to meet your children, Flora. Please bring them next time."

My children, the twenty-somethings, with their creative talents and disorganized lives; would they come here? Would they like it?

I start to hug Jake's father, but he holds out his hand to me. This time I notice how warm his hand is, how tightly his fingers wrap around mine. My mother-in-law stands on tiptoe in high heels to exchange cheek kisses. She wipes away tears. I'm touched.

Jake says, "Thanks, it was great to be home." He uses that word again and I wonder about the meaning of home. Is it where you were born, where you grew up, where you live now, or where you feel something so immensely soothing that you can relax into your true self?

We have a long journey ahead of us. When the plane bumps up and down, I think of wild iris, sea lions, mariachi bands.

Hours later, we drive through tidy rows of grapes, through a dark tunnel of redwoods until, finally, the sparkling Pacific Ocean lies before us. Our cat, Alfredo, greets us on top of the rickety gate. I breathe in deeply, the familiar salty air pungent with aromas of redwood, fir, and honeysuckle. We're home.

The fog blows in. After a week of Midwestern summer, I welcome the cool dampness. Jake goes outside to check the garden. I take off my clothes. My invisible suit dissolves; poppy petals, curls of bark, thorny leaves, and stringy seaweed fall away. I walk outside naked. My husband rests his elbows on top of the shovel handle and gazes at me. He sings an off-tune version of an old Beach Boys' song, "I wish they all could be California girrllss."

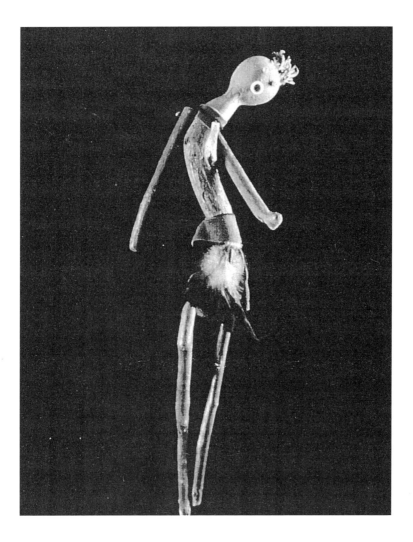

Bury My Heart—Where?

J. J. Wilson

Though I have lived in Northern California for nearly thirty years, every day I am still aware that it is not my native heath. In Virginia where I was born and raised, green is a permanent condition, humidity rises off the trees like smoke, and fireflies light the night. What Californians call "hills," Virginians dignify as "mountains." While I can adjust easily to such differences of scale, certain cultural differences are harder to reconcile myself to.

Here in California, civility seems less emphasized than self-disclosure, and yet no one asks me that telling question, "Who are your mother's people, dear?" In my Virginia family, we observe with both reverence and parody something called "Old Tradish," whereas in California I hear about the need to "invent rituals." For me, rejection of the food I cook is tantamount to being denied citizenship—yet friends of mine here act as if the fried fish and hushpuppies I serve them are a fiendish plot to undermine their health. They also tend to giggle at grits while taking polenta quite seriously.

Some days living so far from where I was born and bred feels cosmetic, and unimportant, some days liberating, and some days downright alienating. Are any Californians brought up in one place or do they all just move on? Change is good, of course, but what about custom?

Perhaps one of the reasons that memoirs have become so popular now is that most people live far removed from their birthplaces. As if fighting a dietary deficiency, we require massive infusions of family histories, memories, gossip, secrets. I was shocked to see a young couple in a Mother Lode antique shop buying family scrapbooks filled with dim photographs of other people's ancestors—reinventing a past they had left behind. I wonder if this craving for memorabilia is an attempt to replace those precious objects thrown from the covered wagons to lighten the load of the past?

The promise and the limitation of California, and indeed of America, is that all of us here are from somewhere else, all immigrants, some more recent than others. But am I condemned to be a perpetual tourist? We new arrivals cruise our "main street," Highway 101, and call ourselves residents of the area, but we are ignorant of the lives that have gone on before we came, we don't know the back roads or the burial grounds. Can we really live a continuous narrative without having buried some of our own dead in this ground?

The obituary notices in the local paper offer me one way of spying on the lives of the "real" residents. The other day I read about "Bobbie" who lived fifty-nine years on a dairy ranch and loved to tell of the day it snowed on her apple trees. There was another account of a "gracious lady" whose special art was making gardens that drew numerous hummingbirds. On the same page, "Pete," a much decorated veteran and "idolized grandfather," had worked as a clerk for Mission Hardware in Sonoma for thirty-two years. We mobile newcomers cannot imagine these settled lives, though we sometimes get an inkling of them at a Grange Hall breakfast or at the Penngrove Fourth of July Parade.

One night at Dinucci's restaurant in Valley Ford, I met a gregarious group of women who told me they had been dining together for forty-five years. They had all worked with each other and begun this pleasant custom because their husbands balked at going out. Some were frail, one in a wheelchair even, but all were dressed for the occasion and clearly enjoying one another's company and their shared history. I envied them.

I had, after all, chosen an itinerant profession. Academics, like missionaries, are likely to be posted to unlikely places. I was thrilled to be hired at Sonoma State University, newly built on the site of a former seed farm. It never occurred to me to wonder what my rights were in this new country. Like the early settlers, the faculty and the students were actually unsettlers, acting as if no one else had ever lived here before we came. We took our welcome for granted, convinced, like other carpetbaggers, that we represented a new and better way of life.

Invited to speak at a Rotary Club on the new concept of affirmative action, I told Virginia Woolf's sad tale about the dire fate of Shakespeare's sister. To my consternation, I saw tears in my audience's eyes. They were mourning the sister literally, taking the fable as fact, and missing my point. I had missed a point too by misjudging my audience's sophistication and ability to play with serious concepts. While I never made just that mistake again, I must have made many others through ignorance of the local culture.

I am still lacking a lot of the stories, the references. Shouldn't there be some kind of a cram course to prepare us for a local-resident test? Sample questions could be: name at least ten local settler families, the tribes that were here before them, the political philosophies of the Penngrove chicken farmers, the crops on which the economy is based (legal and not), community organizations, names of local birds, poisonous plants to watch out for, the dangers of drainage ditches, which roads go through and which do not, etcetera.

Once we had successfully passed this test, we would be given a ceremonial drink at the Washoe House and receive some kind of visa granting us full rights and privileges to live on this land. As it is now, we are in danger of bypassing the existing culture as the new highways do towns, leaving them to gentle obsolescence, with nothing left but chain stores in a kind of freeway-exit generic culture.

Let us rather emulate the settlement patterns revealed in the halfburnt house at Olompali State Park near Novato. Each time someone new came along, another layer was added to the original structure, providing a kind of palimpsest with faint traces of native populations, adobe walls from the Spanish settlers' store, Victorian woodwork, and then a stucco mansion covering it all, until a rock group moved in and started a fire. It is not a pretty sight but then neither are the ways in which the land has been colonized by all of us.

Perhaps I should accept from this multilayered image that change is inevitable and, however ruinous to what has been there before, part of the on-going process of history. Private property is a myth; perhaps the idea of belonging to any one place is also a myth. If I were to go back East (my mother insisted that I always phrase it "back East" and "out West" rather than the other way around), I would not feel completely at home there either. Where is home for people like me? My life lacks that kind of context. No place to call my own, no land I have fought to defend or even to settle, no place to bury my heart.

The Portable Mother

Susan Swartz

It was their first night ritual to stay up late no matter whose time zone they were in, to drink too much, and laugh in the dark. At Jane's house in northern California they sat on the deck, feet propped on the rail, facing the shadowy outlines of the trees that stood around a meadow. The moon thinly outlined a cedar, three redwoods, two Douglas firs, and a row of eucalyptus.

Lily dubbed it the Valley of the Clear Sinus. When the fog dripped through the mulchy mix she said it smelled "like something Mom used to rub on our chests."

The August night was typically cool, and Lily, who came from the Atlantic side of the country, shivered. Where she lived summer nights were sticky and sleeveless.

Jane tossed her an alpaca sweater.

"Which thrift shop did this relic come from?" asked Lily,

who was 10 years older and skeptical of recycled clothing. She wrinkled her nose and examined its purple thickness in the multiple candles on the deck.

"The place with the head lice," Jane laughed, while Lily yanked the wool over her gray curls.

Lily had arrived at San Francisco on the Boston flight with what Jane called, "the Talbot People."

"You dress more like Mom every year," Jane declared, after waving and doing a wiggly dance to get her sister's attention at the gate. Lily had on a celery-colored pantsuit. Jane didn't blend into the background. Currently in her bougainvillea period, she wore a swirl of pink and magenta set off by cowboy boots.

"How can summer nights be so freezing?" asked Lily as she did every visit, now snuggling into Jane's sweater and holding out her glass for more zin.

"What's that?" asked Lily, as the eucalyptus creaked in the wind.

"Mountain lion, probably," said Jane, smirking.

"Very cute, Jane."

At Lily's Rockport home they sat on a screened porch, lit by kerosene lamps. They drank vodka and cranberry juice and listened to the flutter of motor boats returning to the cove.

The sisters, forty five and fifty five, always got a giddy thrill staying up past their normal bedtime although no one in either of their lives monitored their hours. Both rose early; Jane made calls to artists for her gallery, and Lily, a nurse practitioner, had before-breakfast patients at her clinic.

Departing from normal schedules made them feel they were doing something prohibited. Having grown up as well-behaved daughters of an elegant mother, they needed only the slightest alteration to feel like rule-breakers.

The pot helped too. Jane always bought some Graton Gold for her sister's visit and if Lily assumed she did this every night, Jane didn't move to correct the impression.

In Massachusetts, Lily provided Marlboro Lights, snuck from her son-in-law's jacket. Both sisters had quit years ago.

Few ever guessed the two were sisters. When they revealed the relationship they explained they were the two sides of Helen Elliot, their mother. If you put Helen Elliot in between the two, the three matched. Minus her, the two sisters bore little resemblance.

It was a thing with them, to divide their mother into equal parts. They'd had claim disputes over the years about which talents and traits each had inherited. Some were irrefutable. Jane had her mother's smile, Lily, her long legs; Jane had the eyebrows that were usually cocked in surprise and her fear of elevators. Lily had her "lovely round ass" a boyfriend had praised, and the migraine headaches that forced her to quietly exit gatherings and seek a dark bedroom.

As for their mother's style, the sisters took personal liberties. Lily called Jane "aggressively hip." Jane called her sister "steadfastly understated" and bragged that she had inherited her mother's flair.

"I'm the artist. Lily's the scientist," Jane explained. Lily chewed the side of her lip when she heard this.

After their mother died the sisters found that their visits served to keep her around. "Mom travels with us now," explained Jane.

There had been no property or money to divide. Howard, Helen's second husband, had made sure of that. The sisters settled for the parts of their mother that no one else, certainly not Howard, could own.

Shared memory of their mother kept them together because as Lily often told her friends back East and Jane out West, "We disagree on just about everything except Mom."

Helen Elliot had always encouraged the relationship even though the sisters had left their childhood home in Pennsylvania and migrated to opposite coasts for schools, marriages, and careers.

"Jane, you need to call Lily and tell her what a wonderful job she's doing with those kids," her mother would urge. She would send Jane a ticket to Boston and scribble a note on her violet stationary, "My girls need to stick together."

The next year she would send Lily a ticket for San Francisco and again the violet paper and a prod, "Your sister is having a little trouble with her business."

By the time their mother died, the sisters had flown back and forth into each other's lives so often that they continued the annual ritual. One week every summer in California, the next in Massachusetts.

They teased each other about their opposite worlds but privately each enjoyed the bi-coastal experiences. In California,

Lily would crab about sprouts on her sandwich and being dragged to mud baths, and then she would go home and rave to the nurses at work about a fish shack on Tomales Bay where an old seaman barbecued oysters, "so long they look like an appendage."

Jane would go back East and complain about greenhead flies and the pitiful wine selection but return with tales of digging clams at dawn and steaming them in beer on the beach.

"I think we just like to eat the other's seafood," said Lily.

Lily's house had a storm cellar for hurricanes. Jane lived over a major fault and scoffed at earthquake insurance. Jane picketed. Lily sent checks to good causes. Lily attended the Methodist Church where she'd been married, her children were married, her grandchildren baptized and her husband buried. Jane marched to save the redwoods and joined a goddess collective while continuing to read the *Daily Word.*

When they got together they scanned each other for modifications. "Is that a new earring hole?" Lily asked, rolling her eyes. "If you ever need a hearing aid there'll be no room for it. Aren't you carrying this aging hippie thing to extremes?"

Jane zeroed in on a large emerald on her sister's middle finger. "Is this another rock from Greg?" Two years ago, Lily's husband had died and left her very comfortable. She declared she would spend Greg's pension money on extravagances he'd always meant to give her.

Jane encouraged this rare, self-indulgent side of her sister. "It's a small flaw. I like it."

By the third day, their good-natured sisterly sarcasm often slipped into bickering. When it got too heated, they both imagined a scowl forming on the smooth forehead of their mother and returned to being nice to each other.

"I had a dream about Mom last night," said Jane. "She was in a red dress at a grand party. Remember in old movies where butlers are passing around champagne, and people are being witty and dangling cigarette holders? That kind of scene. Anyhow, I walked by a group of people, and suddenly a woman turned toward me. It was Mom. She just looked beautiful and smiled at me. And then she turned back to the others."

"It's like the painting," said Lily, jumping up and walking into Jane's dining room. In the painting, a woman in a white blouse and red shorts was bending down to fix the back strap of a sandal. Their mother had painted it, "Woman in Red," as a student at Penn State. When Jane and Lily asked her who the woman was, their mother said, "I guess I just made her up."

Jane had begged Lily for the painting, assuring her that the English bone china she'd pried loose from Howard was probably worth a lot more. "Besides," Jane said, "You're the one who throws dinner parties. I'm the artistic one." And so the painting came to rest in California.

Every morning Jane said "Hi, Mom" to it as she passed the young woman in red shorts. Jane always had an eye for art. She had turned a struggling arts and crafts store into a small but respected gallery. She'd taken art classes but hadn't shown any particular artistic ability.

Lily didn't tease Jane about art. In high school, her mother had made Lily take voice lessons. But Lily hadn't even made the chorus tryouts and her mother backed off.

Lily, too, loved the red painting. Every visit she sat across from it and had a private reunion, memorizing each curve and shadow to take home with her. Tonight the sisters stood for a long time staring at it. "Too bad she never did anything more than this," Jane said. "She had something."

"She sure did," said Lily.

The next day was a white fog morning. Lily loved Jane's garden best in the ghostly light, the way the lustrous fog sharpened morning edges and colors. She always talked about the rich velvet dahlias. The proud and dazzling sunflowers.

Jane drove to town for Lily's English muffins and when she came back Lily was still on the deck in her pink silk robe and gold earrings.

"So what cultural attraction shall we try today, Lil? There's a new enzyme bath, made out of cedar shavings, where they dust you off with feathers afterward. Another winery? Or there's always the oyster man."

Jane saw Lily close her notebook and reach for her coffee cup. As Jane came closer, she recognized it as a sketchbook.

"What's that?"

"Nothing."

"Come on, let me see," Jane said, grabbing the thick pad and opening it.

"That's my sunflower garden, isn't it?" Jane said. Lily had gotten it with a few deft, subtle lines.

She leafed back through other pages. Lily had added color to these. Shocking, joyful, color. Jane puzzled over a rainbow woman with green legs who twirled in a field surrounded by tall trees.

"How did you do this?"

Lily looked at her shyly. "I don't know. I just started fiddling around one day. Then I took this class because I've cut back my hours at the clinic."

The work was good. It was so good Jane felt a little sick to her stomach. For one moment she even wanted to yell at her sister, "You're not supposed to paint." She started to walk into the house. Then she turned and looked Lily in the face. Lily stared back as hard.

After a long time Jane managed a "Well, well."

"These are very nice. No, they're more than nice." She sighed. "They're in-fucking-credible."

Lily looked up and smiled. "You'll notice I chose green tights over knee-highs."

"I wouldn't be caught dead in knee-highs," said Jane, pouring herself some coffee. She walked over to her sister and held out her cup. They clinked. "To Mom."

Wedding

Suze Pringle Cohan

The September sun shining straight onto her face, Sally rolls over, struggling to hold her web of dreams. Home alone with menstrual cramps, she'd nursed several cups of brandy-laced tea the night before, and fallen asleep on the couch watching a late-night movie.

Her husband, Davie, has been gone three days with his baseball buddies on their annual trip to Tahoe to play golf and gamble. Their twin sons left recently for their first year of college. The house echoes.

She pulls herself from the couch and pads to the kitchen for coffee. Cramps gnaw at her. At this age, shouldn't her periods be lighter?

"I look like shit," she mutters as she examines herself in the bathroom mirror. The bright light makes her squint. Her face is mottled, her eyelids puffy.

Davie said he'd be home by eleven. They are supposed to be at the wedding at one. Searching through her closet for something cheerful, she finds a turquoise pantsuit with shoes to match.

Davie pulls in at 12:30, relaxed and tan. "Hi! How ya doing, hon?" The expected peck on the cheek.

"Just *great,*" she mumbles. "Why are you so late? The wedding starts in half an hour. How was Tahoe?"

"A gas. A total gas. Golfed all day, gambled all night. Even won a coupla hundred. Well, ready to go? What the hell, we're always late anyway." He laughs. "Tahoe was great!"

On their way to Bodega, Davie lights a joint and describes his weekend with the boys. Sally watches the trees go by.

Davie searches for the sports station. "What, dear? I can't

believe they'd plan a wedding at the exact same time as the 49ers game. Can you find it for me? At least I'll hear what the score is."

She wonders who will be there. Probably just Meryl and Randy's relatives and the Sonoma tribe. It'll be fun. She can hide behind her dark glasses and chat with friends.

Sally and Davie arrive at St. Theresa's as the bride and her family assemble in the back of the church. The organ is playing, the air feels humid and heavy, and the church is packed. Davie and Sally have to sit on separate sides of the aisle.

The center aisle is a great divide. Randy's people from Sonoma County are on the right, Meryl's from Los Angeles on the left. The right side is a tapestry of aqua, fuchsia, lilac, rose, and untamed manes of hair. The left is primary colors, calculated lines, and severely styled hair—Chagall and Matisse across from Picasso and Rothko. Sally can't help scrutinizing the L.A. women in the pew ahead of her. One is wearing a backless black dress. A tiny purse hangs from her toned shoulder. The woman, seeming to sense Sally's stare, turns around. Her expressionless eyes and perfect makeup are so unnerving that Sally grins foolishly. Her turquoise shrieks.

The priest finally pronounces Randy and Meryl husband and wife. The congregation spills from the church and friends cluster to visit. The Sonoma County women, looking relaxed, hold their husbands' arms, flick random hairs from their jackets. The men, wearing their suits, look much less comfortable. Davie's best friend, Barry, a large man, pulls at his tie. "This thing's strangling me!" He asks Mary Beth, "Wife, can we take these nooses off now?" She laughs as they both join the others, sharing the ritual review of the kids, jobs, sports scores, vegetable gardens.

Sally sees more women than men in the L.A. group. The woman she'd stared at in the church stands out from the others. She is unusually tall, and her dress clings to every curve. She has starlet's breasts, a tiny waist, sculpted buttocks, and sleekly muscled legs accentuated by platform sandals. She stands like a filly amidst work horses. Lowering her dark glasses, she coolly scans the crowd, slowly studying each man she catches gaping at her. She doesn't seem to see the women.

The heavy church doors open and the couple sweeps down the steps. The crowd tosses rose petals as the newlyweds race for their limo. The L.A. woman strides off toward the parking lot. The guests scatter to drive to the reception.

"You almost tripped down the steps you were so busy looking at her," Sally says.

"What do you mean, dear?"

"You know just what I mean."

"How could I help it, hon? Did you see those knockers? Hey, lighten up. This will be fun. What's the matter? Is it cramps, or just a bad hair day?"

"Both, and more."

Her cramps are a leaden ache. She glances in the car mirror. She still looks awful. Right out of the '50s. Her shoes match. What was she thinking of? Lucky she has her sunglasses to hide behind.

Dense fog shrouds the reception garden in Bodega Bay. It is gray, bone-chilling weather. Dark glasses are out of the question. Her hair starts to frizz and her nose is dripping. She sneezes.

Davie orders a vodka-tonic from the bartender, and he and Sally join his buddies from the Tahoe trip. The L.A. woman laughs in a small group directly next to theirs. Davie looks at the woman over Sally's head.

A friend, Luis, leans towards Sally. "In my country, when there are beautiful women around, we say 'Ah! What beautiful *flores!*'"

Sally glares at him. "This isn't *flores!* This is a Venus' flytrap."

He shrugs and glances back at the woman.

"I bet she isn't wearing a shred of underwear under that thing."

"Hmm," Luis muses.

The air around the woman sizzles. Her hand brushes her date's crotch for a moment, and then moves slowly to her lips. The other men gape; the women look at each other.

Dinner is announced, and the group disperses under the trees to look for their name cards. Sally feels relieved that the guests are geographically separated.

At dinner, Barry elbows Sally and says loudly, "Some chick, huh?"

Mary Beth whispers, "Isn't this a scene? Sort of titillating, having a whore in our midst."

"How can you say that? With all the men, including your husband, practically drooling in their dinners? Who is she?" Sally tries to smooth her frizzed hair.

"Who cares? What's the matter, girlfriend? Listen, you wouldn't be *mad* at Davie if he fell off a cliff. They can't help themselves."

The band has set up on a platform under a big oak and reggae music drifts through the trees. One by one, couples head for the dance floor. As Sally and Davie start to dance, she sees the woman under the trees.

A few minutes later, the woman walks languidly to the dance floor, her date behind her as if on a leash. She pulls him to her and starts to dance. The woman raises her arms over her head. Her dress begins to creep up her thighs, inching up and up.

The bride grabs her groom's hand and hisses at him. Then Randy taps the date's shoulder and the two couples exchange partners. The music slows. With a fixed smile, Randy talks intently to the woman. Sally strains to hear but is too far away. The woman listens, answers, then turns and walks off the floor, laughing.

The wedding rituals continue through coffee and liqueurs, and finally the wedding cake. Meryl and Randy giggle as they feed each other the first bites. Everyone applauds.

"David, we're going for a walk," Sally steers him toward the pond. "I'm so angry I'm almost speechless. That woman has every man here by the balls."

"She's sexy. What can I say?"

"She's more than just sexy, she's using all of you. And you're turned on! It makes me feel old. It shows how distant we've become." She starts to cry.

"Come on, Sal, you know I love you. You're the only one."

He gives her a long, conciliatory hug and kisses her forehead.

"Let's get away next weekend, just us two. Maybe up to Gualala to Barry's beach house," Davie suggests. "We always have fun up there."

"I'd like that," Sally concedes, sniffling. They head back toward the party.

Out of the corner of her eye, Sally sees the woman walking toward the restroom. "I'll be back in a minute," she says.

What can she say? Stay away from our men, you conniving whore?

Sally's hand shakes as she opens the door.

She sees a pair of platform shoes in the toilet stall, but the toes are facing the toilet. She hears a steady stream of water and waits by the sink.

The woman steps out and brushes past Sally to examine herself in the mirror. She lines her lips slowly and blots them.

"Cat got your tongue, honey?" The woman looks at Sally in the mirror.

"Who…are you?"

"Get a grip, sweetheart. Hook, line, and sinker, huh?" She straightens her dress and admires herself.

"You asked who I am?"

"Well, or *what?*" Sally replies. "I just don't believe this." For the first time all day, Sally wants to laugh.

She catches herself in the mirror and sees they are both smiling.

"That's the point!" says the woman. She winks. "Let's keep this our little secret, huh?"

Sally promises she won't tell anyone, except her husband.

Matthewing

Sally Jane Spittles

I love the buoyancy of your step when you walk up the mossy path to greet me. I inhale your belly laugh, feel it rumble way down into my chest, as you watch the antics of our cat, Rafiki.

I love to watch you sleep. You don't leave the earth as I do. I hear your steady breath and know that it will keep me from floating away.

One rainy midnight your father called from New York. Our conversation thinned as he waited for me to pass the phone. I finally had to say, "Matthew has gone for a walk." He paused to muster his fatherly tone. "In the biggest storm northern California has seen in years?" "There is a lull," I said. "He's looking for glowworms; he'll be back soon. I'll have him call you."

When you returned, shaking your head in disbelief, you told me, "You have to see this, there are so many you won't believe it." Helping me on with my coat and boots, wrapping me haphazardly with a scarf, you led me out into the dark. Like children, we each pointed out the tiny lights. We walked along Camp Meeker streets, weaving between the constellations at our feet.

At four one morning you tell me you need to stand in the misting rain and smoke a cigar. Through the kitchen window I see you, content under your wide-brimmed hat. You stand, Matthewing, in a pool of moonlight and watch the smoke swirl into the shadows. I smile at your indulgence in simple things, in smoke and rain and the cool night air.

Venus at Center Forward

Barbara L. Baer

Venus at center forward led them down the field, her long legs flying in a flash of black spandex and pink thigh. The Phoenix pounded after her, women whose hair streamed and breasts bounced under gold shirts, shouting, "Venus! Venus! Go for goal!"

The Phoenix were playing the Barking Dogs, a team known for plowing through opponents like bulldozers. Before the kickoff, Pat, the captain and left fullback, had paced the sidelines nervously. The Dogs' size worried her. Worse, she saw that Kimbo, the Phoenix goalie, was hiding behind dark glasses.

"Venus," Pat said, "Kimbo might be shaky. I tried to get her home last night but she kept ordering one more."

"If she has to barf, send her into the bushes. Then go down on one knee, yell for time out, and move Morgan into the goal." Venus stretched her long legs.

Thank God for Morgan, Pat thought. Morgan stood like a wall at center fullback. Weekdays, she lifted cement bags, built foundations. She also played bass in the After-Shocks, Pat and Kimbo's country band. She played behind Kimbo's quick and quirky guitar, Marianne's drums, and Pat's moody lyrics.

"Dead meat," Morgan yelled at anyone who approached with the ball. "One step more and you're chopped liver." The Dogs would think twice about having to reassemble their parts after a collision with Morgan even if she didn't have Kimbo's agility.

But Kimbo recovered by the time play started. Pat saw her drape her shirt the way she liked it and hoist her sweats at the hips. She'd be in the game.

Pat watched as Venus ran, the ball just ahead of her cleats. She faked, spun, and threaded the needle down the field. She had the center to herself. Pat saw the black and white sphere arch up, hover, and come down into the goal. *Bingo.* Her heart soared.

"We'll score again, then play cat and mouse," Venus told the Phoenix as they huddled. "A macho team like the Dogs is all bluff. They get desperate when they're losing. They self-destruct after five minutes."

The Phoenix women locked arms. "Pheenies! Pheenies! Burn! Burn! Burn!"

Four months earlier, Venus had appeared in the old Monte Rio schoolyard on a hot May afternoon. Pat, Grace, and Kimbo were puffing on cigarettes while their children played on the monkey bars. They saw the tall blond kicking a soccer ball, juggling it on her knees, bouncing it on her thighs, doing a tango step over and back again. Pat didn't take her eyes off the stately woman.

"Come kick a ball," the stranger called. "It's fun."

Pat stood apart, resisting her own curiosity. Kimbo strolled over, ready for action.

"Come on, don't be shy," Kimbo pushed Pat.

"Let me be. I'll watch." Pat stepped back.

"Come on, Mom." Pat's daughters finally pulled their mother into the game. Everyone played keep-away until they fell panting on the grass, all except Venus who still breathed evenly.

"I don't run. I stand or I sit," Pat said. "But I had fun." Her high cheekbones and the tip of her nose glistened. She kept her black eyes hidden from Venus.

"Find some other women and we'll put together a Russian River team," Venus said. "Sunday mornings you'll be running your butts off instead of puffing on them."

Venus was her real name. She told them that twenty years ago she'd made the Olympic trials in the high hurdles, but she'd pulled a hamstring before the games. Pat imagined Venus could still hurdle or even fly; she had the light and supple athlete's body that Pat, built on the heavy side, dreamed about.

"I've never been on any team." Pat lit a cigarette.

"Time to change," said Venus. "You have great soccer legs, and you are good with the ball already. You just need to get in shape."

Pat almost acknowledged that she'd been thinking of jogging again—she had once played handball—but she held back, didn't want to give in so easily.

Venus turned to Kimbo. "You're a natural goalie. You play basketball, right?"

"Yeah, I shoot hoops. I'll find the women," Kimbo said, "but a uniform stinks."

"Wear whatever you want. It's moves that count." Venus looked into Pat's eyes and said to her, "You'll be surprised how fast you'll get back in shape. It beats running."

"Might think of it," she said.

Pat called Marianne, the band's hyperactive drummer. Marianne said she knew women from her gym who liked competition and physical contact. "Remember Trish. She's a runner. She needs a break from her AA meetings," Marianne said. They found a dozen friends looking to try something different, something for fun. Everyone lived on the river year-round, survivors of good and bad times, floods, and tourists. Nobody owned a car newer than 1981.

After the first practice, Pat could hardly walk. "Pain before glory." Venus popped her fist onto Pat's thigh. Later, when she saw the first shadow of muscle definition in her quads, Pat would hear Venus say, "You're a powerful woman and don't forget it. Nature gave you a special page in her book."

Though she seemed to have a particular interest in Pat, Venus never let anyone slack off. She made the women run laps around the school, stretch their quads, then run again until they were panting like puppies, licking salt from their upper lips. Venus ran past them and Pat smelled pine needles, woods after rain. When they became too rowdy doing drills, Venus reined them in. "I'm going to teach you real moves. We'll play with finesse."

By August, four months after Venus had appeared, she'd transformed fourteen women who came in all sizes and shapes, some with muscles stretched and sagging, into a working team.

Pat saw pride in the women, as if they'd absorbed some of Venus' talent.

Kimbo played goalie in her sleeveless sweatshirt and baggy sweats. With her tangled dark curls and big hoop earrings, she looked like Anna Magnani on a soccer field. Long, skinny Trish, their deer-like runner, learned the game but never smiled. Pat, her wide face tanned from working outdoors, her black braid heavy down her back, grew more solid. She pounded the turf and seemed happy playing fullback against the opponents' right forward. When she stole the ball, her teen-age daughters cheered, "That's our mom!"

Venus herself had grown sons, twins. "Sons of my grief," she told Pat. "Or is it grief of my sons?" Pat didn't understand all of Venus' confidences, but she welcomed them just because they came from her. One afternoon, a young man drove Venus' red Mustang to practice. Pat hoped this boy was a son. When she saw the way Venus leaned over to kiss him, she knew he wasn't. All afternoon, Pat couldn't look at Venus. She avoided being anywhere near her.

Before the opening game against the Druids, Venus lay a warm arm on Pat's shoulder. All Pat's resistance melted. She had begun writing her first new songs in over a year about Venus. On a streak, she stayed up half the night, cradling her guitar and singing softly. She worked on a song about a woman made of conflicting elements, one part gold, the other clay. It helped her to write songs, to hear from herself that Venus wasn't perfect. Writing words didn't change anything, but it seemed to bring the unattainable closer; at least it corralled the feeling inside. She wasn't going to play these songs for anyone. Maybe she'd never finish them.

She rose to make oatmeal for her daughters before school, drank her coffee, and headed for the coast, where she put in long hours selling as much smoked salmon as she could while the weather stayed good. From her stand north of Jenner, she looked out over Goat Rock, the Russian River surging into the sea. Her red and white umbrella signaled at passing traffic and people stopped their cars. She emptied her cooler almost every day. She thought of Venus as she watched the sun's glancing, golden rays.

By October, word had spread about the Phoenix. The Barking Dogs dominated the North Bay league and didn't plan to lose their title to novices from the Russian River. They hosted the Phoenix on a small field off the freeway that was riddled with gopher mounds. Most of the Dogs were heavyweights like Morgan, and they had a forward with ice-pale eyes and dragon tattoos on her biceps who bragged she'd never been stopped by a goalie. Kimbo slammed her shots over the post and dived stomach-first onto the turf, clutching the ball. Kimbo's kicks soared up and up to mid-field where Venus trapped the ball, passed to Grace, who passed back to Venus inside. Before the Dogs knew what happened, Venus lined up again to shoot. *Bam.* Three to zero. The Phoenix jumped in a pile. Venus set up two goals for Trish who scored them elegantly. The Phoenix loved every point. The Dogs cursed.

"Look at Trish!" Venus stood beside Pat. "You don't need me."

"What do you mean?" Pat felt a chill.

"You're in charge of your own game now."

"Without you, we'd fall apart. You're our center."

"I may have to leave the river. Be away for some time."

"Why?"

"I'd like to tell you, Pat, I'd really like to, but it's a personal matter."

Pat was still shaken when the final whistle blew.

"Good game, ladies," Venus walked straight toward her car where Pat saw that her boyfriend waited. For a moment, joy went out of the victory. Then Pat noticed Trish standing by the goal. She'd never seen a smile on the thin woman's face. But now she beamed, remembering her glory.

"Get in the car," Kimbo said. "I need a hair of the dog."

"You got it," said Morgan. "This goalie saved our ass and I for one am buying the woman a drink."

"I don't drink anymore," Trish mumbled.

"Let's drive to my place," Pat said. "I've got enough salmon in my fridge for the whole damn league. We can stop for beer and I've got plenty of coffee."

While Grace and Kimbo drank beers on her porch, Pat sliced rosy fish over red onions and listened to Trish tell her she'd never imagined scoring a goal. She said she didn't know if she'd ever do anything so wonderful again.

"You will! Venus has faith in you," Pat said, her own spirits sinking as Trish's rose.

"Soccer's like running wild and free, like running on air," Trish said.

"It's wild all right. You don't know what to expect."

Pat put the platter on her dining room table and watched her teammates make huge sandwiches and praise the day they'd decided to take up sports. Pat wanted to join in and say that Venus should be here to share the fun with them, but she stayed out of the conversation. She wanted to tell Venus that today she'd seen a stillness at the center of the field as everyone was in motion. The team had become a constellation of women in balance, like the Pleiades. She'd seen fluid beauty in Trish, a burnished glow on Grace, focused intensity in Kimbo. Her own hair stuck to her scalp with sweat, her skin was still red from running. She was no beauty, but she saw herself on her page in life, as Venus had said. Venus couldn't be leaving them. She just couldn't.

"Here's to Phoenix! Venus our inspiration, and our captain, Pat." Grace toasted.

"Red-hot and undefeated!" Kimbo wiggled fingers like rabbit ears over Pat's head.

"I hope we stay that way," Pat said. "Remember the Maya in Mexico. They played soccer you wouldn't want to lose. Losers ended up on the altar, hearts cut out."

"Ouch," said Grace.

"Heart of Dog," said Kimbo.

Before their last match, November rains threatened to end the soccer season early. The Phoenix wanted to play in the rain, to slide in mud puddles, to score twice as many goals as the game before. When they arrived at the field to play the Fast Kats, Pat didn't see Venus' red car.

"She'll be here." Pat knew she had to reassure the team even when she felt a churning in her stomach. She'd called Venus all week. No answer. The black sky seemed to rest on her shoulders with the weight of everyone's questions.

Pat made them stretch and then take a lap around the field. Finally, they couldn't stall any longer. Trish cried, "We can't play without Venus."

"Don't be a sissy. That's a giveaway." Kimbo was sober and intense.

Trish looked as if she needed stabilizing. Pat pressed the back of her neck, hoping she'd find her energy point. "You can do it, Trish. We're not going to let Venus down by forfeiting. Until she comes, you're at Venus' position. Center forward."

"Me? I couldn't."

"You have to. We need you, dear." Pat stared into Trish's eyes, making her understand that she had to do it.

The Fast Kats wore orange and black stripes and painted charcoal whiskers on their cheeks as if it were still Halloween. The Phoenix marked their players as Venus had taught them, but when they had their chance on offense, they seemed distracted and their shots flew off the mark. Several times Pat thought she smelled Venus' tangy forest, sweat, and honey scent. She looked up and saw only dark, westward-racing clouds.

When the referee blew the final whistle, both teams crossed to the center, shook hands, then dragged themselves to their cars. The zero-to-zero tie felt as hollow to Pat as if she had been singing her heart out but forgotten to turn on the mike.

As she drove home along the river, rain spattered her dusty windshield. Pat opened her driveway gate. She knew her girls were with friends, but still she hoped that someone would be there.

Pat couldn't get back in the car. Instead, she sat down in the dirt and felt the anger she'd harbored all week toward Venus pour out in the rain. Where had Venus gone? Would she never return to them? Pat feared the answer. During the game, she felt Venus touching her face, whispering goodbye.

Pat trudged inside and began layering kindling in her wood stove. She knelt in her shorts and mud-caked soccer cleats and blew on the sparks. Finally they shivered and burst into flame. She stared into the fire until she saw the golden figure of a woman curving there, rising upward. She chanted *Venus, Venus* to keep the fire going.

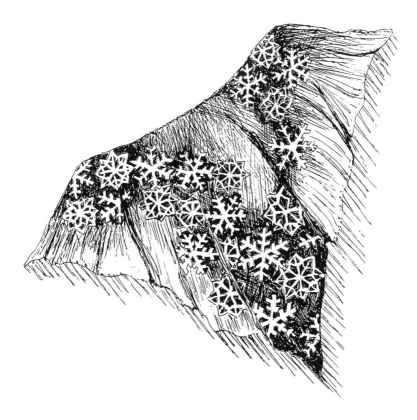

Ancestral Strength

Linda Noel

Winter shimmers before me
lonely. Hip down, shoulder
angled.

I am part my grandfather waiting
for first snowfall before leaving
Willow Creek.

Part my mother who helped
push her father's car from snow-covered
red dirt ditches.

Part my gramma living snowbound
in pine country.

Part my father who walked the miles
to town, sledding supplies back to
gramma's ranch.

Winter draws its shawl about us.
Salmon know to return home.
And mushrooms have found light.

I look into winter and know
that no frost can freeze
the spirit.

No thousand winters of ice
could put out the flaming heart
of our people.

Knots

She drives the highway again.
This season the curves chew the rubber
of her tires

as she screeches and squeals the canyon
carved by a river of eels, a valley of vineyard,
acres of orchards.

She drives the Buick and believes in birds
brought into her path as she rides the ridges,
the river road,

the winding road, riding the white line,
the inside line, broken line, fence line, coast line,
timber line,

telephone line, and the southern light, star light,
neon light, searchlight of her life strung through
the night.

And in the roadside parking lot she does not look
for her love lost nor lick the asphalt of her steps.
She scribbles

and shapes ink into sound and stitches stories
and songs only she can weave into a circle.
And it is about herself,

her survival, her security, her standing, her tomorrow,
her tongue, her trail somewhere sought in the parking
lot light.

And who laughs at the lonely night? The speechless.
And who laughs at lace around the neck of night?
Tenderness turned into knots.

Linda Noel

my Indian baskets, Clarence. You know the baskets my mother gave me just before she died. Did you put them somewhere?" asked Carol, tossing wads of newspaper on the kitchen floor.

"Maybe they're checking out their new digs," said Clarence.

"My baskets have a mind of their own, but I don't feel right unless I know where they are," said Carol.

Carol was moving sixty miles north of San Francisco to Occidental. Clarence, a jazz pianist, was helping her and he was invited to live with her. But, the old redwood cabin with its high ceilings, newspaper insulation, and woodstove belonged to her.

Carol hadn't planned to leave the city but three robberies in less than a year changed her mind. Before 1984 ended, burglars had stolen everything including whatever she had stashed in the trio of Indian baskets—dope, extra stamps, change, earrings. She didn't know why they had left her the baskets, and after the third robbery, she began to misplace them. They would reappear in odd corners and on windowsills like old Easter eggs. Carol worried that someone was sneaking into her apartment and hiding them. One night she dreamed she walked a long way until she came to a river, where she cut twigs off the willows on the banks. When she leaned over and pulled aside some brush, she saw her baskets.

"I have to move," Carol said to no one when she woke up.

"Just a minute," Carol told Dan, picking out a fake tortoise-shell barrette from the black and yellow basket and winding her hair up.

Dan and Carol were going dancing in town. There was nothing serious between them, but more often than not, they wound up in bed on Friday nights. Carol expected nothing more than a next time and a little help when a storm blew out the lights and she needed some emergency dry wood for her stove. Everyone else she knew was either married, divorced, or in therapy, which seemed to her like another kind of marital state.

"Hurry up, Carol," said Dan.

Carol fastened her hair quickly.

"What are you doing?" asked Dan.

"Have you ever seen my Indian baskets?" asked Carol. "My mother collected things all her life. It was a talent I didn't always appreciate." Dan picked up the small red-feathered basket and cradled it in both hands. Carol kept a little ceramic pipe in it.

"I've seen baskets like these before, Carol. I'm sure they're very valuable."

"We paid two dollars for them."

"I think they're Pomo baskets. The Pomos have lived here for thousands of years. You might even be able to find out who made these baskets."

That night Carol dreamed she was searching for a comb because her mother had criticized her tangled hair. "Okay, Mom, I mean Linda," yelled Carol's dream self.

She looked inside one basket and found it filled with acorns. The second basket held tiny red feathers. She peered inside the third basket, anxious to find a comb. She found a photo of her mother gathering twigs near a river, young and pretty.

"I don't know why I dream about those baskets," Carol told Dan the next morning.

"Perhaps they're trying to tell you something," he said sleepily.

A few days later Carol saw a rust-colored station wagon on the edge of Bohemian Highway. "Do you need some help?" Carol asked the old woman standing near the car.

"I'm very thirsty. I waited a long time," said the old woman.

"Get in. We'll go to my house and you can use my phone. I'm Carol."

"I'm Jackie. Nice car," said the small woman, settling into the red M.G. "Mind if I smoke?" Jackie wore a white blouse buttoned down the front and a long red skirt. Her silver-flecked hair was braided and piled on her head like a crown. She looked about seventy-five around the eyes, but her lion-colored skin was smooth and unwrinkled. Carol wondered if Jackie was Indian, but didn't want to ask.

"Not at all. I love second hand smoke. I quit a few years back, but still like to inhale vicariously." A glance at the woman showed she wasn't listening. Smoke filled the tiny car, stinging Carol's eyes.

"Are you almost home?" asked Jackie.

"I live about a mile from here on Redwood Lane."

"I don't know how you people can live under the redwoods. It's dark and cold in the winter, and there's little food to gather in the summer. Though I listen to the stories the redwoods tell." said Jackie.

Carol thought Jackie was a little batty but nothing to be afraid of. They rode in silence. As soon as the car stopped, Jackie popped out, surprisingly limber.

"Where's your man?" asked Jackie as they walked into the cabin.

"No husband. Just me. I've lived here over ten years."

"Your house looks very busy," said Jackie.

Carol looked around. On a round oak table sat the unwashed dishes from breakfast with Dan. She stared at the clutter on her desk: computer, a framed photo of her mother, and a vase crammed with wilting Shasta daisies, the dried petals spilling onto the floor.

"So what happened?" asked Carol. She handed Jackie a blue goblet filled with water and a large crystal ashtray.

"Nice crystal," said Jackie, giving it a quick ping. Jackie lit a cigarette and inhaled deeply. "I spent all morning at the river cutting white willow twigs for my baskets. I'm a basketmaker. I was headed home when the car decided to stop."

"Are you really a basketmaker?"

"My mother taught me basketweaving. She learned from her mother." Carol looked at Jackie's hands. Maybe they were stained by more than nicotine.

"I want to show you something," said Carol. She ran to her bedroom and grabbed her baskets, dumping their contents out on her bed. She placed the trio on the table in front of Jackie. "Linda, that's my mother, gave these to me before she died."

Carol was surprised at how proud she sounded.

Jackie stared at them for a long time. She picked up the red-feathered basket and brushed it lightly against her cheek. Her fingers circled the edge of the canoe-shaped basket. She closed her eyes. "Myrtle, my mother, made these baskets," said Jackie finally. "My mother was a medicine woman. These were stolen from our house many years ago."

"You recognize these baskets? That's hard to believe," said Carol, remembering the greasy man at the flea market. Was he the thief? She walked over to the desk and picked up the picture of her mother. Her hands were shaking. "I doubt they were stolen."

"They were taken from our house in Cloverdale on May 4, 1964," said Jackie. Her cigarette smoldered in the ashtray.

"Well, we certainly didn't take them," said Carol, fanning smoke away from her face. "We bought them at a flea market. Linda always had a knack for spotting fine things. Here's a picture of her with her collection of Limoges. You can see the baskets at the top of the cabinet. We always took good care of them."

Jackie picked up the silver-framed photo and brought it close to her face, studying it carefully. "Looks like she has some Indian, your mother."

Then she put the picture down and held the small round basket close to her heart. "This one with the arrow design was used in the old days to separate edible seeds from wild plants." She picked up the canoe-shaped basket. "This coiled basket is started with three willow sticks and is very difficult to make. It's a good feeling to watch a basket grow from the work of your hands. This one is a good shape for holding long objects like pipes or hair combs. My mother showed this basket in the Booneville fair. I remember the blue ribbon."

Jackie pointed her cigarette at the red-feathered basket, and hummed quietly. "This basket is very powerful and was used in my mother's medicine work. She first saw it in a dream. Then she created it. My mother shot a woodpecker with a bow and arrow to get those feathers. That's not allowed today, of course." A smile crept briefly across her face. "The little acorn woodpecker is sacred to us. They make the acorns come. This basket is powerful and dangerous in the wrong hands.

Carol heard a car drive up. "Your ride?"

"We believe our baskets are alive and we want them to be happy. We feed them and sing to them and make them part of our family. I'll take them home," said Jackie, gathering the baskets. "Your mother was wise to save these baskets. And she was wise to give them to you. They were a peace offering from her, you know. And your dreams led me to them."

Everything was happening so fast. Carol knew her mother would have returned the baskets to Jackie, no questions asked. She stood up and followed Jackie, who held the baskets against her chest. She watched Jackie climb into an old car which then disappeared down the driveway.

Back inside the cabin, Carol stared out the window into the shadows of the small redwood grove. Her house felt empty. She picked up the silver-framed photo. There was Linda, in jeans and a hand-embroidered workshirt, standing proudly in front of her best china cabinet. At the top the three baskets crowned her prized Limoges collection.

I miss you, I miss you, I miss you, Linda. I miss you. I miss you. Mom, I miss you.

A rhythmic knocking broke her trance. On the porch rail an acorn woodpecker rapped at a post, its tiny red-feathered crown sparkling in the sunlight.

Ground Heat

Sarah Flowers

In the sun
I am a ground heat
wild oats
and sweet vernal grass
casting shadows.
Trees etch their presence
over my breast.
Tattoos.
The marks indelible.
The ink of their images
prints a calligraphy
of capillaries
in the sun.

In the sun
I am a ground heat
wetness rising after rain
drifting down roads
traveling drainages and ditches
settling over fields
sifting through hedgerows
resting in hollows
in low places.
A mist
a cloud
passing
with no purpose
other than
stringing water beads
across heads of velvet grass.

Predators and Pagans

Nancy Kay Webb

Lambing Season

When I woke up my hair was frozen. Lying on a mattress in the open back of the truck, I had zipped myself into a down sleeping bag and covered up with a quilt, so I slept warm, but a predawn cold snap crisped my hair.

Alan and I slept outdoors for a week, but they never came back. The dogs. Or dog. Our first night in the field was the worst. Disturbed, apprehensive, we were alert to every sound. The images were fresh on our mind: four ewes lying in their own blood, hindquarters ripped apart, seven dead and dying lambs.

Alan loaded his .22. What else could he do? The ewes' staring eyes were pitiful. After he put them out of their misery, I helped heave the carcasses onto the back of his truck. With my fingers deep in her silver wool, I recognized the bearer of our most magnificent fleece.

Alan doctored the surviving, then, still greatly agitated, said, "I'm going into town." The .22 lay in the front seat.

"Do you expect to find the dog? How would you know him? Do you imagine he's still covered with gore? Or will he just look reprehensible?"

He drove around, looking, interviewing. Wandering dogs? Unattended dogs? He hunted up owners of big ill-mannered dogs. Had any of their animals been out last night? Everybody was sympathetic, but nobody knew a thing.

That first night in the field I felt too unsettled and anxious to sleep well. Moreover, I needed to go into the house every four hours to tend the lamb who had developed pneumonia. Alan was dosing her with antibiotics and I was forcing milk-laced Vitrate down her throat. We bedded her in the living room beside a wood-burning stove where we kept a good hot fire going. Every time I opened the front door, I could hear her wheezing and gasping. She sounded like a locomotive. I would fix a baby bottle, hold her limp woolly little self on my lap, press the hinges of her jaw with my thumb and forefinger to force her mouth open, then, taking care not to drown her, I would squeeze in as many drops as she would swallow. Afterwards I would lay her in her nest of towels, throw another log into the stove, and go back to my bed under the tent of clear, cold, black sky.

After an eon of nighttime, the sky began to glow. Into the house. Utter silence. The gasping had stopped. "Well, that's that," I sighed. I had known the lamb wasn't going to make it, but her death made me downhearted anyway. When Alan came in, I gave him the bad news.

"I'll bury her before breakfast," he said, stooping to pick up the motionless body. Then, "Dammit all to hell, Nancy Kay! This animal isn't dead!" He was thoroughly disgusted with me, and spent the morning muttering to himself, "The animal stops breathing like an Allis Chalmers WC, so it's dead. Right? No other explanation. Can't possibly have gotten quiet because it's gotten well." Oh, me of little faith.

A couple of days later we noticed a ewe, mother of twins, suckling three lambs, two white and one black. It's rare for sheep to voluntarily adopt a lamb, but, as it turned out, this ewe had accepted the lamb because she was too weak to reject it. Examining her, we couldn't believe she was still on her feet. The Hell Hound had mangled her viciously. Starting with the opening of her vagina, he had worked his way in. The external parts of her genitalia were gone, as was much of the surrounding flesh. We put her into a small pen in the goat yard so we could doctor her and give her special feed. Every day we wrestled her to the ground, and Alan flushed out her wounded parts with two quarts of Betadine solution.

We left the male twin with her, but put the two females, along with the lamb from the house, in my vegetable garden where I patched together a small shelter for them. Now I had not one but three bummer lambs to feed. Six times a day I mixed powdered milk replacer with water and heated it in a big pot on the stove. Over the years I had done this repeatedly, but never with more than one animal at a time. At first the primary challenge was juggling three bottles, and making certain the lambs all finished more or less simultaneously, because if one got through too soon, especially if it was the big aggressive ex-adoptee, she would shoulder her way into another's share. I had to manipulate things so that the fastest sucker got the stiffest nipple with the smallest hole.

Later on, when they had grown and, though eating more, ate less frequently, I fed them through the fence, using the wire and my thighs to support the bottles. The challenge then was to keep the lambs from butting the bottles out of my grasp. The bigger they got, the harder they butted. Until the lambs were weaned, my thighs stayed black and blue.

Harvest Moon

Now it is lambing season again. Our pasture is alive with lambs jumping like sand fleas. New lambs mean last year's crop go into the freezer. Today is butchering day.

A heavy sliding door lets us into Vick's shop. The smell, not a dead animal smell, but a healthy, cold, fresh-meat smell greets us. All around the walls hang deer antlers, faceless mounted horns, several wearing loops of used saw blades. The big room has a concrete floor and three large dusty windows. No view, yet plenty of light falls on the ten half-lambs. Pure ivory and coral, they lie side-by-side, slightly overlapping with their straight hoofless legs pointing at the band saw.

Alan and I wrap while Vick cuts. Though Vick is an old man, we can barely keep up with him. How many chops to a package? Shoulder roast or pieces? Shanks? Stew? Ground?

> *Worthy is the lamb that was slain to receive power,*
> *and riches, and wisdom, and strength, and honor,*
> *and glory, and blessing.* Revelations 5:12.

Strength is by way of garlic or sometimes rosemary. Riches are by way of sauce. And the glory takes place between the palate and the tongue.

Each reunion I have with one of the honored and blessed of our flock confirms to me its delectability. One sybaritic reunion, a celebration of a harvest moon, fell on the autumnal equinox. The party was at a friend's house up on the Ridge, where autumn evenings are warm and crickety. Children swam in the pond while their parents, barefoot, drinking wine, and chatting, enjoyed the dregs of a summer season.

Guests had brought salads, vegetable dishes, breads, and sweets to fill the vast outdoor table. In a nearby stand of tall trees, a cast-iron bathtub held a colossal quantity of glowing coals. Cooking the meat took patience. This barbecue patience was paired with the gift for gab, the sweet banquet of the mind. Wit, laughter, flirtation mixed with the fine rich gamy smell of sizzling lamb.

After the food came drums. Harmonicas, guitars, too, but chiefly drums. We danced under the round moon. We danced until the last drummer begged us to set him free. Next morning my feet were bruised and scraped, but that night they stamped and pounded the damp grass with painless joy.

Bridges

Simone Wilson

Cal Corso rounded the last curve on the road to Jenner and saw that another wall of the house was missing. The Morrisons had moved back to the city years ago and abandoned the place. Every year Cal watched as summer sun dried the yellow paint and winter storms flecked it away, until the bare boards held up a skeleton roof. Then the boards began to go away.

Cal drove his pickup down the hill every morning to the post office, and every evening he drove home past the shrinking house. He never saw one of his neighbors pry off a two-by-four with a crowbar, but this summer the north wall of the kitchen had disappeared. Last week the porch supports had vanished, leaving the patchy roof as floppy as a wet hat.

He was tempted to stop the truck near the cypresses and lever off a few boards himself—you never knew when you might get a project going. But he did not want Iris squinting at the yellow flecks. She was huffy about scavenging private property and he did not like to lie. Besides, it was satisfying to just sit back while the house magically erased itself, like watching the waves eat up the bluffs at Portuguese Beach. It was a way of keeping track. If the universe moved that slowly, there was still time for something to happen.

Cal was the postmaster of Jenner, where the Russian River swept by in one final gesture before losing itself in the Pacific. He was also the only postal employee in Jenner, so in addition to sorting mail and thumping letters with the rubber cancellation stamp, it was his job to haul the American flag skyward every morning and take it in for safekeeping at five o'clock. The flag had its own drawer behind the counter, but every afternoon he folded it into a neat triangle and carefully laid it on the passenger seat, where it rode home with him.

Sometimes Iris looked at the flag on the seat, like she knew that seat was taken.

"You ought to have a girl sitting there with you, Cal," she told him one September afternoon. He wondered whether she meant herself. At fifty, his stepmother was only eight years older than he was. When his dad died, he had hoped she would move back to the city with her sister, but here she still was a year later, rooted on the porch that faced west, where on bright days you could see the sea flash between the branches of the blue oaks. She was there in the house and the garden and the porch while his hair thinned and the sun set and the house at the bottom of the hill vanished plank by plank.

That night she fried up his favorite meal—liver and onions with lima beans—then pushed a blackberry tart in front of him. She grinned while he forked it all in, then moved her wooden chair closer to his. Cal kept chewing and thought about stumps he planned to pull up next spring.

After dinner he retreated to the far end of the garden, where the land dropped off sharply to the creekbed. In the failing light Cal could just see the butter-colored meadow across the gully. Beyond that was the old cabin that had been his boyhood hideout.

As a teenager he had built a makeshift bridge over the gully with leftover pickets and scratchy rope, so he could retreat to the cabin even if the creek rose. He spent free afternoons alone there, reading science fiction and shucking the wrappers off Snickers bars. By his junior year he was as hefty as a football player but without the muscle to attract the girls he noticed in silence at the Redwood Cafe.

Then one afternoon, when he was halfway across the gully, the saggy bridge lost heart altogether and gravity had its way. The ropes stretched like rubber bands, and Cal rode the shaky center board down into the cold gloom until he stood on the sandy creek bottom.

Now, as he stood there in the twilight, the meadow across the creek had an inviting silver glow. While liver and blackberries settled heavily in his stomach, Cal looked down at a patch of soft, worked earth where the moonlight cast his pudgy shadow.

On Saturday morning, Iris was leaning against the formica counter, watching coffee dribble into a glass carafe. Out the window, she saw a pillar of dust rise over the shaggy buckeye. Brush fire?

Iris banged out the screen door, crossed the garden, and stopped at the edge of a hole that wasn't there the day before. Cal stood in the pit chopping at the earth like a crazed miner. The next shovelful of earth just missed the scrawny, bare ankles above Iris' pink slippers.

"What the hell is goin' on?" asked Iris.

"Science project."

The next hunk of earth sailed over the slippers and shattered against the trunk of the buckeye.

That afternoon Cal was driving down the hill past Bob Keller's place when he noticed the rusty Volkswagen. He pulled over near the derelict car. Inside the cab, blackberry vines twisted over ripped seats. Cal walked over to the fence, where Bob was pulling nails out of lumber, tossing the bent nails over the fence and clinking the straighter ones into an old Hills Brothers coffee can.

"How about you selling me this VW, Bob?"

"You don't want that car. Engine's shot." He was almost indignant. "My oldest kid, Jimmy, he bought another bug and looted this one for parts. I ought to pay someone to haul it away."

"I really just want the frame, long as the axles turn and the tires pump up." Cal kicked a flaccid tire.

"Trade you for that leftover PVC stacked behind your house," said Bob.

"Deal," said Cal, "if you help me tow it to my place tomorrow."

"Deal," said Bob.

Sunday morning at eight Cal arrived at Bob's with a pump. He had all four tires plump as doughnuts by the time Bob ambled out the back door with his coffee. They hitched the bug to the back of Cal's truck. By the time they reached the Corso driveway half a mile up the road, three tires were nearly deceased. They unchained the battered car, muscled it up the knoll near the buckeye, and set a course for the excavated garden.

Cal and Bob stood behind the rear bumper and gave the VW a good shove. It lurched down the hill, bumping on its three mushy tires and one fat one, and jumped into the hole like a rabbit. The ripped canvas of the sunroof, luffing in the morning breeze, was just visible above the lip of the burrow.

"Sunk in there real good," said Bob. "Now what?"

"Now I get another Volkswagen."

Cal changed into a clean blue shirt and headed through the redwoods to Guerneville. He parked his pickup on Main Street and jogged up the wooden steps of the *Russian River Gazette.*

Alice Warrender sat on a stool behind the counter, editing strips of newspaper copy and tapping the butt of her Exacto knife against the wooden counter. Every now and then she twirled it around and sliced off a few inches of type, tossing the pieces over her shoulder.

Cal eyed the steely little scalpel and cleared his throat. Alice stuck the blade into an eraser for safekeeping.

"I need an ad," said Cal. "How much for how many words?"

Alice recited, "Five bucks for fifteen words, fifty cents each additional."

"Uh, let's see, 'Wanted VW bug with inflatable tires engine no object, Box 18, Jenner 95450.

"That's thirteen."

"Okay, then put, 'Engine no object, write Cal,' and then the address."

"Good," said Alice. "Comes out on Tuesday."

At the hardware store on Church Street, Cal asked Al Bertoli for thirty yards of medium weight cable, eighteen bags of cement, and a Snickers bar.

"That's a lot of cement," said Al. "You expecting a flood up on the ridge?"

"Just shoring up a bank near the house. Don't want to wait until the rains."

"Need any lumber for forms?" asked Al.

"Nah, just the cement. I'll drive around back and load up," said Cal, dropping the Snickers into his shirt pocket.

When Cal got to the post office a few mornings later, he clipped the flag onto the rope, raced his colors up the pole and tied it off with two firm half-hitches. He unlocked the office door and spread the day's mail across the counter. Underneath two copies of *Sports Afield* was a blue envelope addressed to him. He sliced it open and a scent of jasmine rose from the paper. Paychecks from the Postal Service didn't smell like jasmine. They smelled like stale glue.

Dear Cal, if you still need a used Volkswagen, there's one in my front yard on Freezeout Road, fourth house from the bridge on the left. No phone. Come by and see—Sylvia Mistral.

After work Cal drove up Freezeout Road and pulled over at the fourth mailbox. Beyond a navy blue VW in the yard, he saw a porch with two cowboy boots propped up on the railing, toes tilting at the sky. The woman in the boots had long red hair escaping from a knitted cap. She was leaning back in a kitchen chair, reading *Popular Mechanics.* When she saw Cal she draped the magazine over the rail and hurried on over. Close up, Cal saw some grey hairs keeping the red ones company.

"I'm Sylvia. You here about the car?" The force of her deep voice almost pushed Cal back, but its lilt reeled him in. He nodded.

"Frank left it with me ages ago. I thought he would come back for the car if not for me, but neither of us had much hold on him," she said. "The car runs but it needs a new transmission. We both ought to have a major overhaul, I guess. Two hundred sound okay?"

They sat on the porch as Cal thumbed out the cash. The sun fell behind the west ridge while Sylvia scribbled on the pink slip.

"If you want, I'll drive behind you and you can give me a ride back," said Sylvia.

Cal smiled back shyly, stuffing the pink square into his pocket. "Okay."

On Saturday, Cal got up at dawn and rolled a spool of cable across the wet grass. He threaded steel lines through the

sunroof of the sunken Volkswagen and looped them several times
around the rear axle. Then he stirred cement into a porridge.
He had just started pouring it into the car frame when he looked
up and saw Sylvia standing on the little knoll, backlit against
the sky. From this angle she looked like a Teutonic goddess. Cal
felt like a mole, blinking upward, covered with dirt.

"I came over for some tapes I left in the glove compartment,"
Sylvia said, "but now I'm more curious about the fate of these
Volkswagens."

There was no way out. He had to explain, and nothing but
the truth was even remotely believable. Sylvia sat at the edge of
the bank and tucked her legs into the tent of her corduroy
skirt, waiting.

"It's for a suspension footbridge—like the Golden Gate,
only a lot smaller." He felt like a complete idiot.

"And this is what anchors it? Buried cars filled with
cement?" She sounded intrigued.

"The cars are sunk on either side of the creek, with the
cables strung in between," said Cal. "The cement adds more
weight and keeps the cables from working loose." It began to
sound dimly possible. He began to breathe again.

"Iris thought you were making a two-door wine cellar."

"You met Iris?"

"She told me you were down here," said Sylvia. "She
sounded worried about you. Has been for a while. That's why
she hasn't moved back to the city."

"Iris told you that? When?"

"During the third cup of coffee. We've been watching you
from the house."

Cal contemplated burying himself along with the Volkswagen.

"How will you keep the bridge from sagging?" asked Sylvia.

"I drove your VW around the back way to the other side of
the creek," said Cal. "This cement should set by tomorrow, if
the sunshine holds. Then I'll string the cables across the gully,
tie them to your axle, and roll the car backwards into a hole I
dug on that side. That'll stretch the lines tight."

"I'll be back," said Sylvia. "I want to see this."

Late the next afternoon, Cal and Sylvia worked side by
side, sweating and shoving against the bumper of the second

car until it dropped into the pit. The cables stretched taut and twanged like guitar strings.

"Now all we need are slats for the walkway," said Sylvia.

It was dark when Cal and Sylvia parked by the cypresses and started ripping boards from the ragged wall of the abandoned house. When headlights passed by, they crouched behind the wall, giggling like teenagers. As soon as the lights angled out of sight, they tossed the planks into the back of Cal's pickup.

Two months later it rained six inches and the creek rose.

On a clear evening after the rain, Cal and Sylvia sat on the bridge and dangled their legs over the edge, listening to the hum of the radio Iris had left behind.

Waking the Dead

Maureen Anne Jennings

Mr. Cassidy saw a ghost on Railroad Avenue last night. Sensible, sober, Mr. Cassidy swore he saw a wraith of a woman in a long white gown floating across the narrow road. She'd shrieked a horrible scream just before she disappeared, a scream he said made his blood feel like a milkshake. He'd almost crashed the station wagon, but instead turned the car around and drove into Occidental to the Union Hotel for a shot of brandy. With no ice. God forbid the kids and Mrs. Cassidy should see him with shaking hands and a face as ghastly pale as the ghost's gown.

Mr. Cassidy was not a fanciful man.

The news spread through town this morning like one of the big fires every man on the volunteer fire department prayed would never happen. Mr. Rigley, who owned Camp Meeker's only store, had heard Mr. Cassidy describe his shocking experience last night. The store-owner told the postmistress first thing when she went in for her morning bearclaw. Telling the postmistress any gossip was better than hiring a skywriter. Redwoods might block the sky, but everybody had to get their mail.

Tess Fallon swept the porch very slowly as she listened to her mother and Mrs. Cassidy murmur in the precise volume that made eavesdropping on an adult conversation as frustrating as searching for Sputnik in the sky.

Mrs. Cassidy had made cool compresses and been so worried she sent the kids to the beach at ten in the morning, before all the fog lifted. She'd given them five dollars from the saltine tin and said they could buy lunch at the Snack Shack instead of waiting for her to arrive with the tote bag full of peanut butter sandwiches, fruit, and the leaky jar of Kool-Aid. She hadn't even checked to see if Brian had his noseplug or if Peg was wearing one of her dad's old undershirts to protect her from sunburn.

Then Mrs. Cassidy walked over to the Fallon's cabin to borrow some Bisquick for a cobbler. Mr. Cassidy loved cobbler. It was too bad that his days off fell midweek, when all the other dads were working in the city. Mrs. Cassidy smoked three whole Salems while she talked. Seeing her husband so upset scared her worse than the idea of ghosts. The women agreed that if Mr. Cassidy wasn't calmer tomorrow, the Cassidys could visit Father Dermody at Saint Phillip's. The priest could talk to Mr. Cassidy, or maybe even exorcise the road.

How did you exorcise a road?

Tess never got around to asking her friends, either during the long afternoon at the beach while they passed the bottle of baby oil and iodine back and forth, or later during boring Teen Night at the Barn, when everybody just stood around waiting for the chaperones to die and something to happen. There were lots of questions she didn't ask her friends these days.

Peter hadn't been at the Barn; he hated Teen Nights. But he'd promised this afternoon that he'd meet her tonight. If she didn't die herself before she left the house again.

When she raced home with her younger brothers for their cruel 9:30 curfew, the sweet rich smell of applesauce filled the kitchen. It was the first batch this summer, part of a lug of Gravensteins, simmered with spices, raisins, and brown sugar. Mom would heat it for breakfast in the morning, a breakfast for good children who'd slept all night in their safe beds.

"Hi, Mom. Smells good in here." Tess faked a huge yawn and hurried into the chilly bathroom before her mother could reply. She brushed her teeth with water so cold her mouth ached, stole a tiny bit of Oil of Olay, changed into her long white nightie, then retreated to her bed on the porch to pretend to sleep.

Her brothers talked for a minute, and then quieted into their reliable deep slumbers. Tess pulled the flashlight from under her pillow and scrunched down into the sleeping bag to read just one chapter of *Wuthering Heights*.

The cowboy print on the bag's red flannel lining faded into a rosy, moist, Pepsodent-scented shell. Tess read three chapters, stopping every few pages to peek out of her cocoon to see if Mom was still awake. As the batteries weakened, the golden illuminated circle of text shrunk a few inches from her face. She would ruin her eyes. Tess sighed and returned the flashlight to its emergency-only spot under her pillow. Her parents would give her hell if they caught her wasting batteries.

Waste was big on their sin list, but it would be a straight-A report card compared to what might happen if she were stupid enough to take the flashlight with her later. Look, everybody, Teresa Mary Fallon is shamelessly sneaking around town in the middle of the night. In her nightgown.

It was taking centuries to get out tonight. Tess closed her eyes, trying to train them for darkness. Finally, she heard her mother's book drop to the floor and saw the glowing square on the ferns below her window disappear.

Tess studied the sky above the porch, and decided to leave after she counted fifty stars. Then three-year-old Kathleen woke up from a nightmare wailing about clowns and ghosts.

She'd never get out if the other kids woke. Tess tiptoed to the far end of the sleeping porch and carried Kathleen into the cabin. Her sister's arms wound around her neck like the mohair turtleneck she'd wanted last Christmas.

It was a shame to wake Mom again, but she'd couldn't escape with Kathleen's body wrapped around her like a vine.

When the bedroom light clicked on, Tess slipped inside and lowered her sister into her mother's bed. Mom snuggled Kathleen next to her big stomach under the covers. Funny how her mother's face looked so much younger without makeup, while Tess knew the right eyeliner and mascara could make her look at least eighteen. If her parents ever allowed her to wear it.

"Couldn't you get her down again, Tess? You know how hard it is for me to sleep these days. Don't ever get in the family way in the summertime."

Peter promised her every night that nothing they did could give her a baby. She always asked him; he always swore she'd be safe. He was seventeen; he must know these things. Plus, he went to public school, where they learned the important stuff dumb Catholic schools like hers didn't teach.

Tess looked at the alarm clock on Mom's bedside table. Would he still wait? Or walk off somewhere with Monica or Susie, whose mothers let them wear makeup and stay out as late as they wanted?

Peter said almost every night how tired he was of waiting for her to prove she really loved him. He'd said it more and more lately. Last night, he told her she'd better not keep teasing him or expect him to wait forever. Not a very romantic thing to say. It had shaken Tess so much she'd forgotten to tell him about the car that could have killed her as she'd run to be with him. Love shouldn't have a time limit.

"Sorry, Mom, she wanted you. Sweet dreams." Tess pretended to yawn again. Please God, let dreamy Peter still wait in their special place. Let her see him soon. And feel him.

Mom's voice stopped her at the door. "Tess?"

No escape yet. She tried to sound sleepy when she asked what her mother wanted. A just-us-girls chat now could ruin everything.

"Thanks. I couldn't handle the summer alone with you kids all week without your help. I do see what you do, you know. I promise I'll remember to tell your father this weekend."

Tess shuddered. If her parents really saw what she did, she'd be confined to a convent where nobody talked for life.

"Hurry back into your cozy bed now, sweetheart. You're shivering as if somebody's walking on your grave. How many times do I have to tell you you'll catch your death walking around barefoot?"

Catch her death. Catch the devil. Catch hell. They never talked about catching anything good, like kisses, or flowers, or falling stars. No bouquets fell from their somber skies; no friendly signs appeared to guide a girl along a dark path.

Tess' hair almost turned white while she waited for Mom's light to go out again.

She tried to see the road with her feet. The trick was to look straight ahead, focusing about two yards in front of her face. Don't look down. Peer into the near distance long enough, and the dark dissolved into vague shapes and spaces. She'd scream like a banshee if any of the shapes moved.

On a night this dark, it didn't matter if she opened her eyes as wide as a Mary Quant model or closed them like a girl who'd just seen her worst school portrait ever. Last week's moon had provided hazy outlines of the trees and houses she'd snuck past. The week before, she'd been able to see scarves of fog on the upper branches of the redwoods, glowing like her aunt's Spanish rosary beads in a darkened room.

Darkness veiled everything tonight. Tess concentrated, feeling the pavement under her calloused summer soles. The center of the narrow road rose higher than its edges. She tried to read the slight slope with her feet, putting one directly in front of the other as if the rough asphalt were a tightrope. She flinched at every sharp pebble and chewed on her lower lip so she wouldn't cry out. But this way felt safer than creeping along the road's edge, one bare foot on the pavement and the other in the dust and redwood needles. The sword-blade ferns would slash at her legs, while small trees and scrub brushes next to the road grabbed at her body and poked sharp branches at her face. She could lose an eye. Imagine explaining that to Mom in the morning.

It must be practically midnight—way later than usual. Not even the night owls' lights shone in those scattered cabins above the road whose yellow beams served as her secret landmarks. She always held her breath while she crept past those houses, still grateful for their spots on her private map.

Teenage girls were never, ever, supposed to huddle naked in a stand of redwood trees in the middle of the night—not even for a few shivering seconds to shimmy out of a little girl's modest nightgown and into a cute outfit. Tess had hidden her India-print blouse and denim miniskirt in the treehouse behind the Burns' deserted cabin this afternoon. They hadn't used their place in years, not since old Mrs. Burn had a heart attack and died right there on the deck.

Tess rolled her nightgown into a tube the way *Seventeen* said prevented wrinkles, and stuffed it into the brown grocery sack that had held her clothes. The paper sounded like elephants having a potato-chip party. She wondered if Mom would say the noise sounded loud enough to wake the dead, the way she always did when Tess and her brothers fought.

How did you wake the dead?

She needed the bag, noisy or not. Last week, she'd tossed her outfit directly into the treehouse, not even worrying about scorpions. She'd wriggled into her clothes in the usual darkness, then wanted to cry later when Peter laughed at the cinnamon-colored tree dust smearing her pink crop-top. His laugh had been worse than the time Fred threw her into the pool and the kleenex she'd stuffed into the pointy cups of her new bathing suit disintegrated. The tissue had floated up to the surface in little strands that looked like the sperm trying to reach the egg in the Family Living movie last year.

Sucking on a peppermint lifesaver as she walked, Tess finally saw one light winking through the trees from the Cassidys' house. She didn't want to think about them either.

All her favorite books, the ones she had to smuggle out of the library or bookmobile because Mom said she wasn't mature enough to read them, had heroines who risked all for love, including their very lives. The sight of a ghost on a dark road would truly scare her, but probably not all the way to death. Did Peter believe in ghosts?

Her familiar route terrified Tess tonight. She could take a wrong turn and get lost. The trees whispered ugly gossip and swayed toward her as if they wanted to capture her with their branches, acting like strange enemies instead of the old friends she'd known every summer of her life. The thick growth which provided such luscious afternoon shade turned the night roads into chilly catacombs that might be haunted. She kept seeing things out of the corner of her eye, weird, spooky things that disappeared when she tried to focus on them.

She reached Tower Road, the last road before she'd see him. Just down this hill, then into town, where the cleared trees made the parking lot seem like noon. Two more minutes, three at the most. She'd feel safe as soon as she saw him.

Tess whispered a fast prayer that no headlights would race past the blind curve while she dashed across Bohemian Highway, then ran up the post office steps. She stopped at the landing to smooth her hair and tug down her skirt.

She saw a light weaving behind the building. Peter was here, his brazen flashlight throwing spidery shadows through the trees to welcome her. He must have heard her coming, probably been worried she'd taken so long. In one more minute, he'd kiss her. His kisses would banish her lies to Mom, her ghosty fears, all the strange terror of her rush to meet him.

The beam cast a crazy circle high up in the trees and a low, moaning voice said it was time to turn out the lights now. Then a girl's shrill giggle bounced off the redwoods. The noise sounded loud enough to wake a whole cemetery.

In Passing

Susan Bono

I live in a house where ghosts wander. At night they slip light-footed down the narrow hall, pause silhouetted for a heartbeat in my bedroom doorway. I have given up being frightened by the weight of an unseen companion settling into bed beside me, or the jolt of an invisible cat springing onto the covers by my feet. I now regale listeners with the tale of three shy ladies in long skirts peering from a corner, or the spirit so enamored of the guy who refinished the hardwood floors it rode around in his truck for a few days. My stories never fail to elicit shudders from my audience and variations on the question, "How do you stand it?"

The truth is, I don't really know, except that I love my house in spite of the occasional disruptions. Besides, these phantoms do not occupy space needed by my family. They exist along the edges of vision, tangled among the shadows near the ceiling, rovers in that unsettled realm between wakefulness and sleep. Over the last fifteen years, guests who have reported drafts, the sensation of being watched, even apparitions, have rarely been upset by their experiences. This otherworldly element seems as much a part of our house as the breeze ringing the windchimes in the camellia bush, or the fog that chills so many summer mornings. Only the continually shifting identities of these visitors have ever really bothered me. Because everyone's impressions remain so varied, I am led to believe no one group of spirits occupies this household. It feels more like a crowd passing through.

But we are only the third family to live in this house since its construction in 1939. No sordid tragedies have taken place under this roof. While it's true that in the 1970s one of the original owners expired in the bathtub, that hardly seems to account for the wide assortment of characters who have been inclined to put in appearances: the young woman in a neat jacket climbing the front steps, the elderly couple hovering at the foot of our bed, a huge snake twitching its way across the kitchen floor.

It is not the proper house for long-term ghosts, anyway. It is neither grand, gloomy, nor darkly isolated. All day long, the sun turns its slow clock beyond our yellow walls, delivering light at timely intervals through our many windows. The wind, funneled off the white caps of Bodega Bay twenty-five miles away, swirls in under the open sashes and dances in buoyant circles. Nothing can lurk here with a real cat prowling and phones ringing and boys dumping ever-bigger shoes and dirty socks in corners. For a time, an unaccountable mustiness persisted in the back bedroom, but it disappeared a few months after the arrival of our youngest son. I had the feeling my baby's colicky tantrums simply wore out whatever it was. The others only seem to be stopping by for a moment on their way to somewhere else.

These encounters have prompted me to investigate the history of the land itself. The town of Petaluma took its name from a tribe of the Coast Miwoks, who occupied this area for at least ten thousand years. The current population pays little attention to the Miwoks, focusing instead on history that begins with the Spanish ranchers and mission-builders. But my friend's children have reported seeing silent, dark-haired men dressed in skins on the bluffs behind their house. Before roofs and trees obscured the view from what is now Wallace Court, who might have roamed the hill on which our house is situated?

I think of other places those first people walked. A few miles west is the settlement of Two Rock, named for the stone gateway the tribes passed through on their migrations between the Petaluma River and Bodega Bay. Our nearest cross street, Bodega Avenue, often takes me past this landmark, which looks like the broken-off feet of a petrified giant. I try to imagine the land before ranches and asphalt every time I drive by. Certain curves of the blacktop were determined by those who erected the barns and fences, cleared brush, and established eucalyptus, but our main road to the coast must have been built over a much older highway.

Oak Hill Park, which butts up against the houses on our cul-de-sac, was Petaluma's first burying ground. The city never officially annexed it, but before 1866, more than one hundred pioneers were interred there. Settlers often disposed of their dead in ground already sanctified by Native Americans, which may explain why the early townsfolk planted their loved ones among the trees at the top of our steep street. Later, the unprotesting residents of Oak Hill were relocated, but traces of the old graveyard remain. Friends who lived in a turn-of-the-century house bordering the park found bones in their basement. The entire northern slope retains the hushed feel of a necropolis, and seems to resist anyone's efforts to turn it into something different. Some things may want to stay buried.

It seems possible that my family is living near real estate originally intended as a portal between this world and the next, a place that still carries some echo of that purpose, no matter what has been layered over it. While the boundary separating us from the dead may be a membrane that can be permeated at any point, we have heard so often of gateways, tunnels, bridges, fords. Just as roads often evolve from footpaths worn into the land, so, perhaps, are the pathways to heaven made. If the patterned carpets in our house have begun to show wear after only a few years of our family's wanderings, surely the feet of the dead have smoothed their own trails over time. In charts not accessible to the living, Oak Hill might still be considered a point of departure, with our house right on the established route. When the time for this particular journey comes, who would not choose a well-marked way? Residents of any area learn which back roads and side streets make the best short cuts. The sky seems closer here than in the newer cemetery on the north end of town. For those locals impatient to get on to the next piece of business, our hill might continue to provide the best connection.

I ponder such connections whenever I visit the Bloomfield Cemetery, out past the twin boulders at Two Rock. The hill on which it perches may well have provided another vantage point for the long-vanished Miwoks, and is brushed by those same winds which toss the treetops on Oak Hill. From the western edge of the graveyard, the earth falls away under a vaulted dome that seems to hold an entrance to heaven. "There's a land that's fairer than day," say some of the tombstones poking from clumps of wild grasses. It was a common enough sentiment among the Victorians, but here it is as if they had been gazing through a doorway into that dreamed-of landscape. The seabreeze creates updrafts that could lift souls like kites, and set free those not tethered by a loved one's grief. Even the secretive little town tucked at the foot of the burying ground holds the stillness of the next world. There have been no recent burials here, as far as I can tell, which seems a waste of such a lovely jumping-off place. Nevertheless, what remains under the chiseled monuments maintains a link between this world and the next. And perhaps, as in the case of Oak Hill, there are some who still take advantage of its function.

At the Tomales Catholic Cemetery, behind a modern cinderblock chapel, the old graveyard opens like a book whose covers have been forced apart by the wind. While the graves themselves remain anchored to the tilting hillside, old sorrows have been blown from between the fluttering pages, like so many pressed flowers and tokens. I have stretched out on the cement over a plot to let the sun warm my living bones and to remember that no sadness lasts forever. I have run my fingers over the inscription, "All flesh is as grass," while sheep cropped the green of the adjacent pasture.

I come to places like these with my camera, peering through the viewfinder at the smooth, bare arms of statues, the folds of stone draperies, those naked marble feet. Stalking these figures for their most expressive angles, I often feel a gathering stir just beyond my range of vision, hear rustling that might not be the wind or a lizard in the weeds. "Show me," I whisper, as the shutter clicks. Nothing untoward ever slides from the shade of trees or gravestones, no extra radiance is translated onto my negatives. The barrier between worlds remains fixed, but I like to imagine those on the other side stepping a little closer, curious as to my doings. I arrive with picnics, much as people of the last century did, to keep company with my own mortality. When my eyes follow the direction of carved hands pointing skyward, I am studying a map I may one day follow home.

Perhaps that journey will require me to pass through a house not unlike the one I live in now, a place unwittingly built in the middle of an unseen thoroughfare. I may become the musty draft that rattles a cupboard in a closed room, or the dark shape darting through a doorway. And if I am not quite ready to cross the threshold into the next world, I might linger there awhile, breathing in the milky perfume of a baby's blankets, trying to mold the form I've become to fit the shape of a bed or chair. I would never think to do any harm. I might even be surprised to see terror in a resident's face if I tried to whisper some last message, forgetting, as I shed the burdens of my former life, how such visits once frightened me. I might try to tell that person not to be afraid; I am only passing through.

The Authors

Barbara L. Baer worked with women writers and artists to create *Cartwheels on the Faultline*. Between times, Barbara shares a home in Forestville, writes, reads, gardens, plays tennis, swims with her dog.

Robin Beeman lives in Occidental. Her books are *A Parallel Life and Other Stories* and *A Minus Tide*. She teaches writing at Sonoma State University and Sebastopol Center for the Arts.

Susan Bono continues to follow her interests in photography, writing, teaching, and editing. Susan has been editor-in-chief of *Tiny Lights*, a magazine devoted to personal essay, since 1995.

Journalist/author **Eileen Clegg** lives in Bodega Bay with her husband and son, and is still trying to answer the question: "So what do you do with a degree in philosophy?"

Pam Cobb loves change—New York debutante, Kansas motorcycle racer, captain of her own commercial fishing boat for ten years. Today she enjoys writing tales and creating assemblages in Graton.

Suze Pringle Cohan is a twenty-five year resident of the Occidental area. Suze is an exercise physiologist, fitness consultant, runner, yogini, theatre improv student, lover of words, laughter, music, and movement.

Marylu Downing, native Californian, created the cover art and collected illustrations for *Saltwater, Sweetwater* and *Cartwheels on the Faultline*. Marylu's story, "Native," was inspired by marriage to and friendships with transplants.

Peg Ellingson has spent most of the last twenty-four years in Sonoma County raising two children and teaching English at Santa Rosa Junior College. Sometimes she also writes.

Sarah Flowers is a naturalist for coastal state parks and for CNPS-sponsored school programs. Sarah's poems have appeared in many publications.

Other stories by **Mary Gaffney** are in *Cartwheels on the Faultline, Travelers' Tales Brazil*, and Copperfield's literary review, *The Dickens*. This year she'll complete a novel. Really.

Joyce Griffin, retired Santa Rosa Junior College instructor, spends her time writing, painting, sculpting, gardening, and in Russian River environmental work. Joyce lives with her husband at Hop Kiln Winery.

Maureen Anne Jennings contributed a story to and edited *Cartwheels on the Faultline*. She is currently writing her second mystery and a book about Proust. Maureen's work will appear in *Travelers' Tales Italy*.

Michele Anna Jordan has written ten books, including *California Home Cooking* (Harvard Common Press, 1997). She hosts "Mouthful" on KRCB-FM, writes a column for *The Press Democrat*, and received a 1997 James Beard Journalism Award.

Marilyn B. Kinghorn, her husband, David, and daughters, Jessica and Haley, made their home in Graton for over thirteen years. Marilyn and David are forever involved in scriptwriting.

Glory Leifried has lived in Sonoma County all her life, except for a brief period in Germany. Glory is a mother, a preschool teacher, and a student. She is interested in the issues that concern people of color and children.

Bobby Markels is a thirty-year resident of Mendocino. Bobby has published many stories, poems, and articles, and five books: *The Mendocino Malady* series; *Popper*; and *How to Be a Human Bean*.

Bonnie Olsen McDonell used to paddle her surfboard to work on Monte Rio Beach. Twenty-five years later, Bonnie is a family nurse practitioner with three kids, living, working, and writing in Sebastopol.

Delia Moon is a grandmother, godmother, lover, and investor. Delia lives in a creek meadow near a buckeye tree, where she plays music, draws pictures, writes poetry, and counsels psyches.

Doris B. Murphy, an animal lover, a licensed clinical social worker, and a community activist, is currently writing her memoirs, which include the political turmoil of the '30s, '40s, and '50s.

Linda Noel is a Native Californian of the Konkow Maidu tribe. Linda resides in Mendocino County.

Noelle Oxenhandler's poetic essays appear regularly in *The New Yorker* and other journals. She and her daughter, Ariel, live in Glen Ellen, where Noelle runs a private writing workshop.

Fionna Perkins first published poetry in San Francisco in 1936. Her fiction and poetry appear in five anthologies and several journals. She and her husband live on a wooded acreage on the Mendocino coast.

Sara Peyton fled Boston in a blizzard by Greyhound and came to San Francisco to visit her sister in 1977. A freelance writer, Sara lives in Occidental with her husband and two sons, and still dreams about snow.

Liza Prunuske is co-owner of an environmental restoration business in Occidental. She would rather dance than clean her refrigerator any day.

Author of six books, **Salli Rasberry** self-published a best seller at the age of thirty. Visual artist, international consultant, and environmental activist, she practices living her life out loud. Sally's friends call her eco-babe.

Robin Rule, 1989-90 recipient of the California Arts Council Fellowship in Literature, is the author of six books. She is the publisher and senior editor of Rainy Day Women Press in Willits.

Karen Eberhardt Shelton is a vegetarian with Celtic roots, a poet for life, mad about fresh air and rural byways. She has a daughter from India and a dog named Camelot and is waiting for humanity to grow up.

Miriam Silver, a journalist, figures she is forever caught between the east and west coasts. Miriam is the mother of a toddler boy, the surest thing that ever happened to her.

Sally Jane Spittles has published stories in *Aene Literary Journal* and *Sailing Magazine*. She edited *Aene* for one year. Sally hosts monthly open readings at her Graton café, the Willow Wood.

Ginny Stanford is a nationally known artist whose paintings are represented in private and public collections. Her prose was first published in 1995, in the *New Orleans Review*.

Jane Kennedy Stuppin writes poems about pomegranates, oranges, oboes, harpsichords, and less tangible objects—the color blue, gravity, truth. Jane lives in Sebastopol with her husband, Jack, and son, Jonathan.

Sunlight lives in Mendocino County, where redwoods are close to everyone's lives. "View from a Tree" is fiction inspired by Redwood Summer and the Albion Nation Uprising in Enchanted Meadow.

Joanne Surasky moved west from Philadelphia in 1986, and joined Robin Beeman's group to write fiction in 1992. Joanne worked in advertising, teaching, rehabilitating old houses, and raising a family.

Susan Swartz is a nationally syndicated newspaper columnist and mother of daughters. Susan believes she could have been a hippie had she not grown up in New England.

Patti Trimble is a poet, educational writer, artist, musician, environmentalist, and mother who lives in Sebastopol.

Christy Wagner, whose writing is widely published on the Mendocino Coast, has taken a leave from teaching to travel while earning an MFA in Creative Writing from Antioch via the internet.

Marianne Ware, fearless autobiographer and practicing irreverent, is 61-years-wise and congenitally witty. Marianne teaches at SRJC, is the recipient of an NEA grant, and is roundly published.

Lynn Watson teaches creative writing workshops in Sonoma County. Lynn's books of poetry include *Amateur Blues* and *Catching the Devil*. She is currently working on a novel.

Dee Watt swims with her dogs and other friends in the Russian River, rides horses, and is privileged to walk on many life journeys in her work as a psychotherapist.

Nancy Kay Webb has been farming and writing on the North Coast since 1980. "Predators and Pagans" is taken from her recently completed book of essays.

Annie Wells received the 1997 Pulitzer Prize for Spot News Photography. She is a photojournalist at *The Press Democrat*. Her work is in the permanent collection of the National Museum for Women in the Arts, Washington, D.C.

J.J. Wilson, a native of Virginia, has lived in Sonoma County since 1969, teaching at Sonoma State University in the English Department and traveling Sonoma back roads for fresh views. "More of a reader than a writer."

Simone Wilson dabbles in every form of writer's procrastination, from hiking worldwide to desktop publishing. She is the author of *Sonoma County, The River of Time*, and has received five national awards for film reviewing.

Though **Jane Zacharias** honors the beauty of the North Coast, this writer also owes homage to the bricks of Boston, the sherries of Spain, and flashes of red cardinal wings in a snowstorm.

Judi Bari, best known as an environmental activist, began her political work as a union organizer for postal workers in Washington, D.C. She came to Sonoma County, worked as a union carpenter, and saw firsthand the effects of logging old-growth redwood. While sanding a redwood board, Judi understood the importance of saving the old trees. In 1990, she was bombed by an unknown assailant and then arrested by the FBI. Until days before her death from breast cancer March 2, 1997, Judi worked on her lawsuit against the FBI for false arrest. The case remains open. Judi's friends and colleagues continue the fight to clear her name. *Timber Wars* is a collection of her journalism, speeches, and interviews. Judi Bari is survived by two daughters, Lisa and Jessica.

Suzanne Lipsett was born in Buffalo, grew up in the Los Angeles area, attended U.C. Berkeley, and moved to Petaluma with her husband, Tom Rider, in 1985. She edited other writers' books for many years. At forty, she began to publish her own fiction: *Coming Back Up; Out of Danger;* and *Remember Me*, nominated for the Bay Area Book Reviewers' Association Award and the Pen West Literary Award. In *Surviving a Writer's Life*, Suzanne described the education, revelations, and the complex demands of writing and leading a full life. In 1996, while battling cancer for the third time, she worked on *Across Death* with Suki Miller, and a collection of personal essays, *Non Believer: An Atheist Seeks Her Path*. Suzanne is survived by her husband, Tom Rider, and two sons, Sam and Evan.

The Artists
and Photographers

Artists

Susan Amato	Woman Waiting	142
Maggie Ballard	Up River	14
Michelle Bellefeuille	Pacific, North Coast, 1977	65
Inge Borgstedt-Nevins	Mouth of the River	76
	Coleman Valley Road	212
	Tree Tops, Willow Creek	226
Janet Bradlor	Seated Nude	78
Elfi Chester	Walk in the Park	16
	Child with Penguin	58
Tamsen Donner	Black Iris	75
Marylu Downing	Saltwater, Sweetwater	cover
	Trees	42
	Rabbit in Shade	132
	Graduation	148
	Flora	169
	Venus	194
Carol Golden	Thinking of Cigar	192
Peg Marrs	Beach	96
	Octopus	97
	Shawl of Winter	202

Miriam Owens	Kelp Couple	103
	Dancer	176
Ginny Stanford	The Painter Returns to Her Senses	26
Elizabeth Ryder Sutton	Susan	9
	Waiting with Othello	68
	Potluck	181
	Detail from Potluck	186
Allis Teegarden	Woman as a Beach	24
	Three Baskets	207, 208, 211
Elaine Vickery	The Woman in Red	51
	Kenwood Landscape	160
Don Williams	Resurrection	86
Victoria Wagner	Brown Trout	240

Photographers

Susan Bono	Foot	234
	Angel	239
Karen Eberhardt Shelton	Cows in the Laguna	126
	Apple Trees	130
	Sheep in the Fog	214
Michael Eschenbach	Portrait of Salli Rasberry	79
Doris B. Murphy	Goblin as Pup	139
Salli Rasberry	Sunflowers	104
Tom Rider	Suzanne Lipsett	4
Renee Robinson	Spirit Sea	title page
	Bridge, Mendocino	110
Annie Wells	Michele	82
	Rescue	84
Nicholas Wilson	Judi Bari	33, 36

Acknowledgments

We would like to acknowledge the presses and publications where writing by the following authors has appeared in part or in its entirety.

Judi Bari, *Timber Wars,* (Monroe, Maine: Common Courage Press, 1994.) Permission from the author.

Bobby Markels, "Going to the Where?" *Coast Magazine,* Late Summer, 1997.

Robin Rule, *The String Creek Saga,* (Willits, CA: Rainy Day Women Press, 1997.) Permission from the author.

Ginny Stanford, "Death in the Cool Evening," *Broken Mirror,* 1997; *The Portable Plateau,* 1997.

Sunlight, "View from a Tree," *The Mendonesian,* August, 1996; *At Our Core: Women Writing About Power,* (Watsonville, CA: Papier Maché Press, 1998.).

Christy Wagner, "Bon Ami, Mon Amour," *Mustang, Je t'aime,* (Gorda Plate Press, 1996.) Permission from the author.

Photo acknowledgments:

Tom Rider for photograph of Suzanne Lipsett on page 4.

The Press Democrat, Santa Rosa, for photos by Annie Wells on pages 82, 84.

Nicholas Wilson for photographs of Judi Bari on pages 33 and 36.

Order Form

Floreant Press
6195 Anderson Road
Forestville, CA 95436
Telephone 707.887.7868

Please send me ———— copies of
Saltwater, Sweetwater at $13.50 each.

Please include $3.00 shipping and handling for the first copy
and $1.00 for each additional copy.
Californians: Please add 7.5 percent sales tax.

Name ————————————————————

Address ———————————————————

———————————————— Zip ————